PETER AND THE STARCATCHER

A Play by **Rick Elice**

Based on the novel by
Dave Barry and Ridley Pearson

ACTING EDITION

For information, address Disney Editions, 1200 Grand Central Avenue, Glendale, CA 91201.

ISBN 978-1-4231-8434-8
FAC-025438-21316
First Edition
10 9 8 7
Printed in the United States of America

disneybooks.com
peterandthestarcatcher.com

SUSTAINABLE
FORESTRY
INITIATIVE
Certified Chain of Custody
Promoting Sustainable Forestry
www.sfiprogram.org
SFI-01054
The SFI label applies to the text stock

Peter and the Starcatcher was commissioned and developed by Disney Theatrical Productions and produced at New York Theatre Workshop (James C. Nicola, Artistic Director & William Russo, Managing Director), February—April 2011. This production trans-ferred to Broadway and opened on April 15, 2012, at the Brooks Atkinson Theatre, where it was presented by Nancy Nagel Gibbs, Greg Schaffert, Tom Smedes, Eva Price, and Disney Theatrical Productions. The production was conceived and directed by Roger Rees and Alex Timbers, with music by Wayne Barker, movement by Steven Hoggett, scenic design by Donyale Werle, costume design by Paloma Young, lighting design by Jeff Croiter, sound design by Darron L. West, music direction by Marco Paguia, fight direction by Jacob Gringolia-Rosenbaum, dramaturgy by Ken Cerniglia, technical supervision by David Benken, casting by Jim Carnahan/Jack Doulin/Tara Rubin, press by O&M Co., general management by 321 Theatrical Management, assistant stage management by Katherine Wallace, and production supervision by Clifford Schwartz. The cast was as follows:

BLACK STACHE	Christian Borle
MOLLY	Celia Keenan-Bolger
BOY (PETER)	Adam Chanler-Berat
GREMPKIN/MACK/SÁNCHEZ/ FIGHTING PRAWN	Teddy Bergman
MRS. BUMBRAKE/TEACHER	Arnie Burton
SLANK/HAWKING CLAM	Matt D'Amico
SMEE	Kevin Del Aguila
PRENTISS	Carson Elrod
ALF	Greg Hildreth
LORD ASTER	Rick Holmes
CAPTAIN SCOTT	Isaiah Johnson
TED	David Rossmer

The understudies were Betsy Hogg, Orville Mendoza, Jason Ralph, and John Sanders. The musicians were Marco Paguia (conductor/piano) and Deane Prouty (drums/percussion).

Originally Presented as a "Page To Stage" Workshop Production by La Jolla Playhouse, February—March 2009
Christopher Ashley, Artistic Director & Michael S. Rosenberg, Managing Director

"To have faith is to have wings . . ."

When I came on board as playwright, Roger Rees, Alex Timbers, and Disney's brilliant dramaturg, Ken Cerniglia, had already hit on a great organizing principle. Act One would take place on board two ships at sea—all cramped quarters, tiny cabins, claustrophobic, dark, wet, sinister. Act Two would take place on a tropical island, with bright sky and big, open spaces. In order to create a simple, stark environment in which to tell a young person's story in an adult, muscular, and surprising way, the directors embraced the style of Story Theater, or Poor Theater—a favorite technique of Alex's and the trademark of Roger's great Royal Shakespeare Company triumph, *The Life and Adventures of Nicholas Nickleby*. The dozen actors would play everyone and everything—sailors, pirates, orphans, natives, fish, mermaids, birds . . . even doors, passageways, masts, storms, jungles. They would also narrate action and memory, giving each of them a privileged relationship with the audience. This would encourage the audience to be more than spectators; it would invite them to play along, to participate, to imagine.

The early workshops of the play gave me great faith in their concept. I aimed to write a play seasoned with the contemporary, irreverent tone of Dave and Ridley's *Peter and the Starcatchers* and the stylistic flourishes employed by J. M. Barrie a hundred years earlier for the original *Peter Pan*—high comedy and low, alliteration, puns, broad physical gags, songs, meta-theatrical anachronisms, sentiment delivered so deftly that the end of the play breaks your heart. My challenge would be to write this new play in such a way that it merged the two disparate styles but also connected the dots between the now-mythic characters and plot points of Barrie's original with Dave and Ridley's reboot. The marriage of classic and modern in the writing brings the Story Theater aspect of the play into sharper focus. And the Story Theater style gave me the freedom to create a vast landscape of far-flung places, physical and emotional. And the wings to take you there.

—Rick Elice, 2014

CHARACTERS

THE ORPHANS

Boy (Peter): A boy who doesn't miss much. Nameless, homeless, and friendless at the beginning of the play and a hero by the end. A survivor. More than anything in the world, he wants a home and a family. If he could grow up, he'd fall for Molly in a big way. But it'll never happen.

Prentiss: Ambitious, hyper-articulate, logical; yearns to be a leader, even as he knows in his heart that he never shall be one. A bit of a blowhard with just the teeny-tiniest touch of cowardice.

Ted: Obsessed with food: the eating of, the fighting over, the dreaming about. A natural actor, an easy wit, perhaps a future poet. Called "Tubby" by Prentiss, though not due to girth, of which orphans, given their meager diets, have very little indeed.

THE BRITISH SUBJECTS

Lord Leonard Aster: The very model of a Victorian English gentleman, loyal subject to the Queen, devoted father, faithful friend. Also, and not irrelevant to our story, Lord Aster is a Starcatcher—dedicated to protecting the Earth and all who dwell thereon from the awesome power of starstuff.

Molly Aster: A true leader at a time when girls are mostly followers. Will risk everything for the sake of Doing Right. Curious, intelligent, beginning to feel things she doesn't yet understand—romantic longings that revert to childish tantrums under pressure—because, after all, she's a thirteen-year-old kid. She'll be a great woman one day.

Mrs. Bumbrake: Molly's nanny. British to the bone. Still has enough of her girlish charm to turn a sailor's head and leaven his dreams. Stiff in the lip, loose in the hip, fun on a ship.

Captain Robert Falcon Scott: Captain of Britain's fastest frigate, the *Wasp*. Years later, he will lead an expeditionary team to the South Pole, freeze to death, and become the iconic British hero, Scott of the Antarctic.

Grempkin: The mean and malodorous schoolmaster of St. Norbert's Orphanage for Lost Boys. Likes to keep his boys in the dark, as sunlight is known to feed rebellious notions, and on account of the preference in certain quarters for lads that are white and pasty.

THE SEAFARERS

Bill Slank: The *Neverland*'s vicious captain, without the skill or quality to lead anyone but himself, and always into disaster. A greedy bastard who'd sell his own mother for a ship to command and send boys to their doom for the favor of those who would use starstuff for personal gain, global domination, or worse. An orphan, too.

Alf: An old sea dog. Something about him appeals to the feminine sensibility—might be his bowlegs, his saucy gait, or his kind heart.

Characters

Mack: A very bad sailor who wants to be anywhere but under the thumb of Bill Slank.

Black Stache: Long after everyone else got out of the pirate business, Black Stache continues to terrorize the seven seas in search of a hero worthy of his villainy. Famous for his face foliage, he started shaving at age ten, had a bushy handlebar by eleven, and the blood of twenty crews on his hands by twelve. Heartless and hirsute, suspiciously well read, partial to the poetical and theatrical, and given to a ferocity from which no good shall ever spring.

Smee: First mate to Black Stache. Single-mindedly dedicated to his captain's every whim. His motto: "'Tis good to be busy."

Sánchez: A hardworking Spanish pirate with an identity crisis.

THE NATIVES

Fighting Prawn: King of the Mollusks, son of Jumbo Prawn and Littleneck Clam. Kidnapped by British sailors and brought in chains to England, he served as sous-chef in a country estate in Derbyshire, where, for no good reason, he learned Italian wines and mastered Italian cuisine. Since returning to his island kingdom, he vengefully murders any English with the temerity to land on his Mollusk Isle domain.

Hawking Clam: Son of Fighting Prawn and Sweet'n'Sour Shrimp. One day, he will ascend the Clam throne as head of the Royal Clam Clan.

Teacher: Formerly a salmon, now an ancient, knowledgeable mermaid.

CASTING NOTE

Actors doubling in roles is terrific fun when it serves a dramatic purpose, and this play was conceived with specific doubling in mind. For example, the actor playing Grempkin and Fighting Prawn (two sources of anguish) doubles the roles of Mack and Sánchez (two victims of abuse). The actor playing Slank (who abuses Mack) in Act One doubles as Hawking Clam (neglected by Fighting Prawn) in Act Two. The actor playing Mrs. Bumbrake doubles as Teacher, a coup which seems to give the audience particular delight. (We chose to cast a male actor in these female roles, so that the actress playing our hero, Molly, would be the only female in the cast, thereby reflecting the isolation of females in general, and young girls in particular, during the reign of Queen Victoria—a time when a woman had the top job, but all other women were expected to be seen and not heard.) Finally, since the point of the play is a celebration of "all"-ness (see the final scene), all the actors should serve variously as sailors, seamen, seafarers, orphans, pirates, mermaids, Mollusks . . . and narrators. In those cases where the actors are narrators, character names accompany the attribution for clarity.

Act One

PROLOGUE

A Bare Stage

*A COMPANY OF MEN enters with a purpose, the
BOY in the middle.*

Boy   When I was a boy, I wished I could fly.

Prentiss   Me too.

Scott   So did I!

Boy   Out the window and over the trees –

Smee   – high as a cloud and lighter than air –

Molly   *(pushing through the MEN)* – then loop the loop and
up to the stars! I dreamed about flying all the time. *(off
the looks from the MEN)* What? Girls dream.

Boy   Up to the stars – I like that.

Molly   Me too.

*A moment of connection between them, the first of
many.*

Aster   Eventually, of course, we dream other dreams.

Prentiss   We change.

Ted   We grow up.

Aster   It always happens. Nothing is forever.

Boy   That's the rule.

Molly   Everything ends.

Stache   And so our story begins.

> *STACHE claps his hands twice quickly. The lights change.*

Smee   Supposing all these planks and ropes are now the British Empire . . .

Aster   And we are lords —

Scott   — and captains —

Molly   — mothers —

Prentiss   — orphans —

Alf   — sailors —

Stache   — pirates —

Fighting Prawn   — tropical kings.

Scott   And use your thoughts to hoist the sails and deck the ships awaiting us this early, gray, and misty dawn in 1885 —

Aster   — a crucial year in the reign of Her Majesty, Queen Victoria —

All   GOD SAVE HER!

Slank   — who, by her grace, had only just knighted a new peer of the realm —

Aster   — Lord Leonard Aster, dedicated minister to the Queen and devoted father —

Molly   — to Molly Aster, whose mother flew up to heaven when Molly was six years old.

Mrs. Bumbrake   In the years that followed, a nanny was employed to care for Molly, and provide her with the essentials of young womanhood —

Aster   — while, taking her with him on each royal mission, Lord Aster gave Molly a life few girls would normally know —

Molly   — a life that made her insatiably curious,

2

insufferably bright, and pretty much friendless at school.

> *PRENTISS and TED seize on that, poking vicious fun at the BOY.*

Prentiss Friendless! Ha!

Ted Friendless? You mean like –

Boy Leave me alone!

> *GREMPKIN, their schoolmaster, is suddenly, brutally, on them.*

Grempkin Orphans! Most useless creatures on earth. Look at 'em –

Slank – cast out by mothers who can't feed 'em or love 'em.

Boy No mothers at St. Norbert's, only schoolmasters.

Grempkin *(grabbing the BOY by the scruff of his neck)* Much as I hate to lose you, mule – *(to PRENTISS and TED)* and you, and you – I won't stand in the way of opportunity. Here's to yer trip on a ship!

Ted What ship? What trip?

Prentiss Sorry, I'm lost.

Ted Me too.

Molly Boys!

Prentiss, Ted We're lost!

Molly BOYS!

Stache And so it was, on the brink of a new adventure –

Prentiss, Ted, Boy – that three filthy orphans –

Aster – and Lord Leonard Aster –

Molly – his friendless Molly –

Mrs. Bumbrake – and her nanny, Mrs. Bumbrake –

All JOURNEYED AT DAWN TO THE DOCKS OF PORTSMOUTH!

> *A hubbub while two trunks are carried downstage.*

Alf – where two trunks are delivered to two ships, sharing the very same dock!

Smee Two trunks, deliberately similar to each other in their . . . trunkness.

Aster One of them, containing a precious cargo belonging to the Queen –

Stache – to be accompanied by Leonard Aster, aboard one of the ships, a spanking new frigate –

Scott – commanded by Leonard's old school chum, the legendary Robert Falcon Scott. Captain of . . . the *Wasp!* *(A model of the* Wasp *appears and is passed briskly along to him.)* Fastest ship afloat. Bound for the remote kingdom of Rundoon!

> *SCOTT, now holding the* Wasp, *beams with pride. The OTHERS applaud.*

Slank *(pushing through)* And the other trunk, full o' sand, courtesy o' me, Bill Slank, captain of this other ship – *(Someone holds up a model of the* Neverland.*)* The *Neverland.*

> *EVERYONE scoffs and groans as the unimpressive* Neverland *model is passed along.*

Stache The *Neverland* – a slower ship –

Smee – and long in the poop.

> *The* Neverland *model arrives in ALF's hands in time for:*

Alf – a merchant ship, taking a longer route to Rundoon, just to be safe.

Slank And while nobody's lookin' – *(EVERYONE turns away, occupied elsewhere.)* I'll just mark the Queen's trunk, the one s'posed to go on the *Wasp. (makes a chalk X on the top trunk)* Then, at the last sec –

Scott ALL ASHORE WHO'S GOING ASHORE!

Slank – I'll switch 'em. *(smacks the chalk-marked trunk)* Get this trunk on board the *Neverland*, y'garbage!

Grempkin And I'll sell these boys into slavery. *(to the BOYS)* Cheer up, lads – you're off to Rundoon, to be helpers to the King!

Slank *(aside, to GREMPKIN)* Food for snakes, more like. *(pays GREMPKIN for the boys, then hollers to his crew)* Crate o' boys comin' aboard!

Scott MAKE YER COURSE! SAY YER G'BYES!

Prentiss G'bye to who?

Ted There's nobody who cares.

Boy Which is why I hate, I hate, I hate grown-ups!

Alf STOW YER CARGO! START YER PLAY! ADIEU! ADIEU!

> *MOLLY and MRS. BUMBRAKE help ASTER into his coat. The other men become MERCHANT SAILORS, ordered about by SLANK.*

SCENE ONE

The Neverland—*On Deck*

> *SLANK cracks his whip and the SAILORS scurry.*

Slank Stow that trunk in my cabin, y'salt junkies!

Sailors *(singing)*
THERE'S WIND IN THE FORETOP,
THERE'S BOYS IN THE HOLD –
TO ME WAY, TO ME WAY HI-HO!

Slank Swabbers to the manacle!

Sailors
OH, THE FORETOP'LL SWELL,

5

THE BOYS'LL BE SOLD,
OR IT'S DOWN, OR IT'S DOWN WE GO.

Slank   Shroud the hemp and jigger the futtocks!

Sailors
OR IT'S DOWN, OR IT'S DOWN WE GO!

Narrator Alf   With everything safely aboard, final preparations are made on the deck of the *Neverland*.

Trimly uniformed BRITISH SEAMEN march on, accompanied by a military cadence.

Seamen
CALL ALL HANDS TO MAN THE CAPSTAN,
RUN THE CABLE DOWN THE CHROME.
HEAVE AWAY, AND SAY G'BYE, BOYS,
FAR FROM ENGLAND, FAR FROM HOME.

The SEAMEN snap to attention, smart and neat.

Narrator Seaman Prentiss   A squadron of British Navy seamen in bright, smart uniforms boards the *Neverland* –

Narrator Seaman Greggors   – led by one Lieutenant Greggors, ready to accompany Lord Leonard Aster to Her Majesty's vessel, the *Wasp*.

GREGGORS wears a naval officer's hat. The Neverland's *ragtag sailors stare jealously at the grandeur of these navy sea dogs.*

Greggors   Captain Scott's compliments, your Lordship . . . but could you join him aboard the *Wasp* as soon as possible!

Aster   A moment. Captain Slank!

SLANK emerges from the shadows, whip in hand.

Slank   Here, yer Lordship.

Aster   I'm taking the Queen's treasure to Rundoon aboard the *Wasp*, but I leave a more precious cargo here on the *Neverland*. Guard her well. *(gives SLANK a gold coin, calls)* Mrs. Bumbrake, bring her to me! *(MOLLY runs to ASTER's outstretched arms.)* Molly, my Molly.

Molly   Please let me come with you. I don't like it on this ship.

Aster   You're safer here on the *Neverland*. By the time you arrive in Rundoon, I'll have completed my mission, and we'll be together again.

> *The ship's cat sidles up to MOLLY's legs, meowing affectionately.*

Molly   Look, Daddy – the cat, the ship's cat. A lucky sign! Here, puss, puss . . .

Aster   Molly! Careful!

Molly   It's all right, Daddy. Him's a sweet little puss, isn't him . . .

> *The cat mews sweetly in MOLLY's arms.*

Mrs. Bumbrake   Our Molly loves all God's little creatures.

> *MRS. BUMBRAKE hands the purring cat to a passing SAILOR.*

Molly   *(ever so bravely)* Daddy . . . I know you don't need my help in Rundoon, but I've got to start pulling my weight sometime.

Aster   You're all grown up, aren't you.

Molly   I am, Daddy. Courage now, promise?

Aster   Promise.

Molly   *(giving in to tears)* Oh dear.

> *Two SAILORS topple a crate very near to Molly's head.*

Narrator Slank   Just then, the crate of boys bursts open!

7

Narrator Boy   One of the boys almost falls out!

Narrator Molly   Hanging upside down just over Molly's head!

Narrator Boy   He stares at her.

Narrator Molly   She stares at him.

Narrator Boy   He has an air about him.

Narrator Molly   The look of a boy who doesn't miss much, or say much about it.

Slank   *(lifting the BOY back into the crate and slamming it shut)* Back in the box, y'monkeys!

Narrator Molly   Something about the boy makes Molly feel like she just grew up a little.

Aster   *(confidentially)* Daughter. *(MOLLY can't take her eyes off the BOY, fascinated.)* A word. *(His stern tone snaps MOLLY to attention.)* There isn't any treasure in the Queen's trunk, and what *is* in it has to be destroyed, by order of Her Majesty, Queen Victoria.

Molly   God Save Her.

All   GOD SAVE HER.

Aster   I'll have to move quickly before the King of Rundoon even knows I'm there.

Molly   But how are you going to destroy it?

Aster   Can you keep it a secret?

Molly   I can.

> *EVERYONE ELSE on the ship crowds around them to eavesdrop.*

All   WE CAN.

> *To avoid being overheard, ASTER speaks in Dodo.*

Aster   *(holding an amulet in his hand, ad libs)* Cwah cheep wirp reet reet burp.

Molly   *(speaking with great difficulty)* Click . . . bleep . . . cwaaaah!

8

Aster   Sorry?

Molly   *(being brave about messing it up) Click bleep cwaaaah?*

Aster   I think you mean –

Narrator Stache   They're speaking in Dodo, a language known only to, well –

Narrator Scott   – dodos – and a handful of very special humans.

Narrator Aster   Dodo: a fat, clumsy bird, hence the Latin name, *Didus ineptus.*

Narrator Alf   Known for its greedy appetite, slothful pace, and sense of entitlement, the dodo was fearless of people and faced no real competition – an eerie mirror of the British Empire at its colonial zenith. Of course, those same traits were responsible for the dodo's extinction – an eerie mirror of the British Empire *after* its colonial zenith – but thereby hangs another tale.

> *ASTER has placed an amulet around his neck and a matching amulet around MOLLY's neck.*

Aster   . . . and don't ever take this off or let anyone else touch it. You know what's in this amulet, Molly. And you know how to use it if you're ever in trouble.

Molly   But what if something happens to you? You need me on the *Wasp.*

Aster   Too dangerous – I won't have it.

Molly   I want to be part of the mission!

Aster   If you can't be British, you can go straight home and back to school, young lady. Mrs. Bumbrake –

Molly   NO! Don't send me home, please. I'll be good, I promise.

Mrs. Bumbrake   Shut the faucet, Molly – blubberin' like a whale when the world's your oyster! Be a woman!

Molly   Yes, Nana.

Aster   Soon as I'm done in Rundoon, we'll take a few weeks in the Antipodes – scare up some rare bird eggs, hmm? I might even teach you to speak Porpoise.

Molly   Yes, Daddy.

Aster   There's my little Starcatcher.

Molly   Just an apprentice. If I were a Starcatcher, I'd be on the *Wasp* with you!

Across the deck, SLANK twitches.

Narrator Slank   Slank hears that word, "Starcatcher" –

Narrator Greggors   – but a cannon is fired from the deck of the *Wasp*!

We hear a cannon's BOOM!

Aster   Patience, daughter. Keep a keen eye, Mrs. Bumbrake!

ASTER signs an autograph for one of the SAILORS.

Mrs. Bumbrake   Don't you worry, my Lord! We'll be British to the bone!

Aster   We'll meet again in Rundoon. God's speed!

Slank   Off ye go, Yer Lordship. TTFN. *(waves cordially as the SEAMEN march ASTER away to the* Wasp*, then to MRS. BUMBRAKE)* Comfy, are we? That's nice. Now – *(suddenly and terribly evil)* Alf, where are ye, ye good-for-nothing bucket o' scum!

Alf   Here.

Slank   Lock these two in their cabin for safekeeping. I'm takin' no chances.

Mrs. Bumbrake   Wait just a –

Slank   I don't fancy no dainty daughters roamin' my deck. Now, hop it!

Mrs. Bumbrake   With pleasure. The cabin could smell no worse than you.

Act One: Scene One

Molly Can we have kitty with us?

> *MOLLY picks up the sweet cat, which now screeches, as terribly evil as SLANK. MOLLY, startled, drops the beast, which scurries down into the bowels of the ship.*

Slank Steer clear o'the pussy, pet – rip yer hand clean off. *(pulls MRS. BUMBRAKE by the elbow)* Say the word, madam – I might let y'out later for a promenade. Maybe do some petting of our own, eh?

Mrs. Bumbrake Don't trouble yourself, I'm sure. Come along, my girl.

> *ALF steps in. MRS. BUMBRAKE likes what she sees.*

Alf It's all right, ma'am. Alf'll see you safely stowed.

Mrs. Bumbrake Thank you, kind sir.

Alf No, thank *you*, kind lady. Yer eyes're green as the sea . . . and yer hair's almost as wavy.

Mrs. Bumbrake *(a girlish toss of her head)* Take me below, sir.

> *MRS. BUMBRAKE sniffs spitefully at SLANK. ALF leads her off with MOLLY in tow.*

Slank Lock the silly cow in the Junior Suite! *(The SAILORS snigger.)* What're you sniggerin' at, y'picaroons?!? Put that trunk in my cabin! *(cracks his whip)* Furrow the jib an' let fly the frammistan, or you'll curse the day you were born! *(The* Neverland *casts off from the dockside.)* On to Rundoon, y'fungus! There's profitable trade to be made in Rundoon!

> *SLANK laughs meanly. The SAILORS moan.*

SCENE TWO

Molly's Cabin

MOLLY and MRS. BUMBRAKE are crammed tightly in the "Junior Suite," a very tiny cabin. The lonely sound of a fiddle wafts by.

Mrs. Bumbrake First Class ain't what it used to be. 'Course, back in my salad days, I was a green girl bringing up brats in a big, breezy brownstone in Brighton. That was a tight spot, too, and hell on the household help. Especially the kitchen boy – a lovely island lad who cooked a cunning cannelloni, plus a pasta fazool to make you drool. But oh, it made the master mad how the mistress moaned fer 'is manicotti. He beat that boy something brutal, but the boy didn't say boo. Point is – we must button our beaks and be brave like that boy, or my name's not Betty Bumbrake. Now, you might well be afraid you'll never clap eyes on your father again, and it cuts me to the core, but never show that sorry Slank the slightest sniff of fear. There are men who can smell it on you, Molly, and they make you pay . . . *(breaks down blubbering)*

Molly That's a stupid example if you're going to cry halfway through. Be a woman!

> *MRS. BUMBRAKE recovers herself as the door flies open. ALF pops his head in and sets down a bucket.*

Alf Situated, miss?

Mrs. Bumbrake *Missus* Bumbrake. Missus.

Alf Sorry to hear that. I was wed once – dreadful business.

Mrs. Bumbrake Mister Bumbrake fell off the twig years ago. Left me widowed at fort – er, *thirty*.

Molly *(notices the bucket)* Is that food? I'm awfully hungry.

Alf This ain't fer no ladies. It's fer the pigs down the other end.

Molly Pigs? Really? May I help you feed them?

Mrs. Bumbrake My Molly loves all God's little creatures, you know.

Alf Not these creatures, she don't. But don't despair – Cook's layin' on some yummy meat in the galley. I'll escort you when it's up.

Mrs. Bumbrake Nothing too rich, pray. We girls must watch our waistlines.

Alf Been thinking 'bout getting in shape, me-self.

Molly Round is a shape.

Alf Sorry?

Mrs. Bumbrake So true. You're quite the specimen.

Alf No, I have flabby thighs. But fortunately my stomach covers 'em. Best be off. *(passes gas)* TTFN.

> *ALF exits but forgets, in his flirtation, to lock the cabin door.*

Mrs. Bumbrake He's rough, but he's ready, that Alf.

Molly He smelt like smelt.

Mrs. Bumbrake True . . . but there's a whiff of hero about him, mark my words.

> *MOLLY pushes the cabin door, which swings open.*

Molly Left the cabin door ajar. I could follow him and feed the piggies! May I, Nana, please?

> *Not waiting for an answer, MOLLY bolts out of the cabin.*

Mrs. Bumbrake Molly, come back here. Don't make me

come after you! *(turns green as the ship creaks and the cabin lists)* Oh. Oh dear . . . *(calling off)* Best bring back a bucket before Betty Bumbrake blows her bloomin' breakfast!

SCENE THREE

Bowels of the Ship

> *Careful not to be seen, MOLLY follows ALF down the dim and damp gangways, passing MACK and another SAILOR.*

Mack C'mon up for some poker, Alf?

Alf Slank put me on pig duty, the rat bastard. Goin' down to the bilge to feed the swine. *(MOLLY follows ALF through a swinging door and down another cramped passageway, both of them on their knees. ALF breaks wind in her face.)* God Save Her.

> *ALF goes one way, MOLLY another – jumping down a hatch into the bowels of the ship. Darkness and dripping. There are many doors to many cabins. MOLLY opens a first door and finds a mob of gamblers. After a frenzied roll of the dice, and much shouting, MOLLY slams the door shut. She makes her way down the gangway. Behind a second door, worshipers gather in prayer.*

All *(singing)*
ETERNAL FATHER STRONG TO SAVE,
WHOSE ARM DOTH BIND THE RESTLESS WAVE,
WHO BIDD'ST THE –

> *MOLLY slams the door shut. She makes her way to*

a third door. She opens it to find SLANK wielding a branding iron over MACK'S hand.

Slank I said *port*, you idjit! *Port!* Which way is port?

Mack The right! The right!

The other SAILORS cringe.

Slank Left, y'fool! Gimme his left! A nice big P – help you remember!

SLANK brands MACK's hand with a giant letter P – a horrible hissing of burning flesh. MACK howls. MOLLY slams the door shut. The ship's a scary place, but she's not afraid.

Molly Pigs!? Where's the pigs?

MOLLY spots ALF and follows him through one final, wretched door.

SCENE FOUR

Bilge Dungeon

Three filthy urchins, the BOYS from the crate, huddle together. MOLLY slips in behind ALF and stays hidden by the door.

Alf If it ain't the three little piggies! Got yer sea legs?

Prentiss, Ted Oh thank you! Get us out of here! Hungry! Please! Help!

Alf *(shutting them up)* Oi!!

Prentiss Excuse me, sir. Quick question for the Captain –

Alf What are you, piggy spokesman?

Prentiss I'm the leader.

Ted No, you're not.

Prentiss Yes I am. I'm the oldest.

Alf I'm the oldest and I say pipe down.

Ted But I'm hungry!

Alf It's yer lucky day then, ain't it?

> *ALF throws TED the bucket.*

Ted Finally!

Alf You'll wanna swallow that down quick. Bone uppity.

> *TED devours the contents.*

Prentiss Any good?

> *TED gags and spits out a glob of slop, choking.*

Ted IT'S ALIVE!

> *PRENTISS peers inside the bucket.*

Prentiss It's worms!

Ted He fed me worms!

Prentiss I won't eat that.

Ted *(to ALF)* Please, sir – is there a vegetarian alternative?

Alf In my day, pigs weren't quite so particular.

> *ALF starts to leave. The BOYS fight over the worms.*

Prentiss Don't hog it all. Gimme!

Ted You said you wouldn't eat it!

Boy *(can't stop himself, to ALF)* YOU! WAIT!

Prentiss *(hissed, to the BOY)* What're you doing!?

Ted You'll get us a beating!

Alf *(turning proudly)* Belay that "you"! I'm called *Mister* on this vessel – mark of respect for a lifetime of seafaring.

Prentiss *(to ALF)* Never mind him. He's got a real problem with authority.

Alf Ha! So do I. *(softens)* I know worms is rough vittles, boys, but they'll grease the pipes 'til we set yer down in Rundoon.

16

Boy *(another tack)* A question, Mister?

Alf One.

Boy Do we have to stay down here in the dark?

Alf 'Til Slank hands ye over to King Zarboff.

Boy Is the King nice to his helpers?

Alf That's two.

> *ALF exits. The door slams shut behind him.*

Ted I got a sick feeling about this.

Prentiss I'll think of something.

> *MOLLY steps from the shadows.*

Molly No you won't. *(The BOYS scream, terrified!)* In my experience, boys are sadly slow thinkers.

Ted What is it?!

Prentiss What *are* you?

Molly I'm a girl.

> *They edge away, the BOY hiding behind TED and PRENTISS.*

Prentiss No way.

Ted We saw a girl once –

Prentiss – headmaster's daughter.

Ted It was nothing like you. It was all – *(characterizing that awful girl of yore)* "aarrgh, rowrrr, gonna getcha!"

Molly *(the boss)* Who's the leader here?

Prentiss Who wants to know?

Molly Molly Aster. Doctor Pretorius back home says I have an extraordinarily high level of brain power.

Prentiss If you're so smart, how come you're stuck on this dirt bucket?

Molly I'm not stuck. I'm going to meet my father in Rundoon. He has important things to do.

Prentiss We have important things to do.

Ted No we don't.

Prentiss I'm the leader, and I say we got some things.

Boy *(to MOLLY)* He's not the leader.

> *MOLLY recognizes the upside-down BOY from the crate.*

Molly You.

Boy You.

Molly How old are you?

Boy How old are you?

Molly I'm thirteen.

Boy I'm thirteen.

Molly Wait – I just remembered today's my birthday. I'm fifteen.

Boy If you were thirteen and today's your birthday, you'd be fourteen.

Molly I only celebrate odd-numbered birthdays.

Prentiss Wait a minute, wait a minute, doesn't matter how old you are! I'm still the leader. The leader has to be a boy.

Molly *(to TED)* Hey – up our end of the ship we get served proper food. I can lead you there – *(to PRENTISS, pointedly)* which would make me the leader.

Ted *(drooling)* Proper food? Really?

Molly Just tell me your names.

Boy Why should we?

Molly *(conspiratorially)* Only that . . . if you have names, they serve you meat.

Ted TED! I'm TED!

Prentiss But I call him Tubby, 'cuz he's food-obsessed.

Ted I am not food ob –

Prentiss D'you write poems about pie?

Ted To pass the time –

Prentiss Hide beans in your blanket?

18

Ted It's a blood-sugar thing.

Prentiss Faint at the merest whisper of – *(to MOLLY, gleeful)* get this – *(back to TED)* sticky pudding!

Ted *(faints to his knees)* Sticky pudding, it's so good . . .

Prentiss Like I said, food-obsessed. I'm Prentiss. I'm in charge here.

Molly *(turns to TED)* Ever notice, Ted – the more you claim leadership, the more it eludes you?

Ted *(to PRENTISS)* Oh, snap!

Molly And what are you, boy?

Boy *(rudely)* Leave me alone.

Molly Sorry.

Ted Don't take it personally.

Prentiss He's rude to everybody.

Ted It's why he gets beatings.

Prentiss And why he's got no friends.

Ted Go on. Tell her your name, why don't you?

PRENTISS and TED laugh cruelly.

Molly What's so funny?

Boy Thanks, Ted.

Ted He doesn't have a name.

Prentiss Been orphan'd too long to remember.

Ted Grempkin calls him –

Ted, Prentiss *(mocking)* – mule!

Boy Go on! You and your stupid names go follow some stupid girl.

Prentiss Like we need your permission, friendless.

Molly *(defending the BOY)* Doesn't cost any more to be nice, charmless.

Ted What about the food?

Prentiss *(to MOLLY)* You can be like temporary leader – but only 'til we eat.

Molly   *(to the BOY, fascinated)* Fair warning, boy – I shall expose you utterly.

Narrator Grempkin   As no one had ever shown the slightest interest in him before, the boy's eyes began to sparkle and the lure of competition wiped some of the misery from his face.

Molly   Right. Follow me.

MOLLY exits the bilge dungeon.

Ted   Right. Follow Mother –

Boy   Molly.

Ted   That's what I said. Follow Molly.

TED and PRENTISS exit, leaving the BOY alone. The ship groans. The BOY quickly gets frightened, claustrophobic.

Narrator Boy   The boy may have wished to be alone, but he didn't really mean it. The sparkle in his eyes fades, and strange sounds in the dark make him remember the orphanage, make him think about –

Grempkin   WHERE'S THAT MULE!!

Flashback: St. Norbert's Orphanage for Lost Boys. Many ORPHANS stand shivering in a cold, barren school yard. GREMPKIN holds sway, brandishing a wooden switch.

Boy   Here, sir.

Grempkin   *(grabs the BOY by the scruff of the neck)* You are all shades of nasty, mule. Oi – lookit this filth!

Boy   *(knowing what's coming)* Don't hit me, sir! Cesspit's dirty work!

Grempkin   A mule afraid of his own shadow. Be a man!

Boy   Thank you, Mister Grempkin.

Grempkin Uncover yourself, disgrace to the mother that left you!

Narrator Bumbrake *(singing gently)*
OH, FOR THE WINGS,
FOR THE WINGS OF A DOVE . . .

Grempkin *(pointing viciously to another boy)* You watch, or you're next!

> *GREMPKIN freezes.*

Narrator Aster At the mention of Mother, the boy heard a wisp of a song he could barely remember —

Narrator Alf — and saw a shadow of a home he hoped he might have.

> *Instantly, we see a tableau of a happy family — the BOY, embraced by a mother and father and brothers.*

Narrator Stache Father and son —

Narrator Molly — mother and child.

Narrator Smee And even with so little ground for hope —

Narrator Boy — still he believed —

Narrator Prentiss — despite his distress and sorrow —

Narrator Ted — that one day such a home would be his.

Boy *(happy)* Home.

> *The tableau melts away, and the BOY has bared his back to GREMPKIN, who looms over him, wooden switch raised high.*

Grempkin Orphan Rule Number One!

Boy Life is meant to be horrible.

> *GREMPKIN whips the boy hard!*

Grempkin Rule Number Two!

Boy There are no orphans in heaven.

GREMPKIN whips the boy again!

Grempkin   Rule Number Three!

Boy   Missus Grempkin's ugly!

> *The other ORPHANS laugh rudely.*

Grempkin   *(his fury knowing no bounds)* Anyone who laughs is dead!

> *GREMPKIN chases the ORPHANS away. The flashback fades, leaving the BOY alone and whimpering in the bilge dungeon.*

Boy   Mother. Mother . . .

> *MOLLY opens the cabin door.*

Molly   C'mon, you! Last chance! We Asters do not leave boys behind.

> *The BOY wipes his eyes and runs after MOLLY.*

SCENE FIVE

The Wasp—*Captain's Cabin*

> *Crammed in a doorway are ASTER, GREGGORS, and the SEAMEN.*

Narrator Greggors   We shift our attention now to the other ship, barreling due south at a brisk twelve knots. That fine British frigate –

All   – THE *WASP* –

Narrator Aster   – where Molly's father, Lord Aster, has been ushered roughly below deck.

Greggors   Captain Scott's cabin, Your Lordship. Do go in.

> *GREGGORS pushes ASTER inside. The cabin is*

quite dark. A tattered Union Jack covers something large and unidentified.

Aster   Awfully cramped for a captain's quarters.

Greggors   No frills on a frigate, sir. Sánchez, pull the door to . . . There's a good fellow.

The SEAMEN crowd into the cabin.

Aster   Where's the Captain, Lieutenant?

Greggors   *(smiles modestly)* I'm no lieutenant. I told a lie.

Aster   Unthinkable – British never lie.

Greggors   Well, pirates do. Don't we, boys!

GREGGORS throws off his British naval hat, revealing his true identity: SMEE. The SEAMEN reveal themselves as PIRATES.

Aster   I demand to see Captain Scott!

Smee   Why didn't you say so? *Presto Scotto!*

SMEE lifts the Union Jack to reveal CAPTAIN SCOTT, trussed like a chicken with a gag in his mouth.

Aster   What? Robbie! *(to SMEE)* How dare you, sir? Release this man!

Instead, SMEE strips ASTER of His Lordship's coat.

Smee   I'll take the key to that treasure trunk o' yours.

Aster   You'll have to kill me first.

Smee   *(eyeing his two prisoners)* We were going to kill you second, but I'm flexible.

Stache   *(from off)* A-choo!

Immediate terror.

Pirate Alf   He's coming aft!

Sánchez   In a nasty mood!

Pirate Boy A *foul* and nasty mood!

Aster What are you playing at?

Smee "Pirates," sir. The *Wasp* is now a pirate ship. Yer British crew's in chains below!

Aster There've been no pirates in these parts for a hundred years!

Smee We've been keeping a very low profile.

Aster And you're the Captain, I suppose?

Smee I, sir?

Aster Aye, sir. You, sir.

Smee No, sir. Not Smee, sir.

Aster Smee, sir?

Smee That's me, sir. But no Captain I, sir.

Aster You lie, sir.

Smee Oh no, sir. The devil himself's in charge hereabouts.

Aster The devil, you say.

Smee The Prince of Darkness. Our Satanic Supervisor. Foul and Nasty with the Cloven Hoof.

Aster And how would one identify him in a crowd?

Smee By his legendary cookie-duster, that's how!

Aster Whiskers?

Smee By his celebrated mouth-brow, that's how!

Aster Well, does he have *a name*?

Smee The pirate captain they call . . . BLACK STACHE!

The PIRATES shriek and bemoan the hearing of this terrible name. And suddenly, there he stands – THE BLACK STACHE, carrying a bucket . . . into which he pukes and spits.

Stache *(waving cordially to ASTER)* Hallo. *(The PIRATES shriek again and bemoan what might happen next. STACHE continues, winsomely.)*

24

Oh, to be in England, now that April's there,
But whoever's not in England gets to see
  my facial hair.
(to ASTER) Now, you're likely wondering: can the
fellow before you be entirely evil? Can no compassion
un-crease this furrowed brew?

Smee Brow.

Stache Brow. Well, fret not, *mon frère* – I'm a romantic!
There's a poet in these pirate veins, and so I plug into
the muse. *(holds his hand out to SMEE for a manicure)*
But what to do? Which style to use? Iambic? Box office
poison. Haiku? Samur*AI*-don't-think-so! *(suddenly
vicious to SMEE)* Mind the cuticle, Smee! *(Eureka!)*
Hoopah! Got it! *(a steely glare at ASTER)*
A pirate with scads of panache
Wants the key to the trunk with the cash.
Now, here's some advice,
Tho' I seem to be nice –
I'LL CUT YOU!!! Slit you up one side 'n' down the
other so ye can watch yer own stomach flop around on
the deck. *(holds a straight razor to ASTER's throat, but
ASTER doesn't flinch)* I say, Smee – you did explain to
my Lord that I'm a bloodthirsty outlaw?

Smee Aye, Cap'n. But he still wouldn't give up the key!

Stache We haven't got all night, Smee. People have paid
for nannies and parking. Stand aside. I'll have to do
it myself, or I'm not – I'm not – *(heartbroken)* WHAT
AM I??

Pirates BLACK STACHE!!

Stache They refer, of course, to THIS! *(The PIRATES
gasp!)* The trademark nose-brush of every man,
woman and child in me family, dating right back to

the amoeba. Yet, for us, the face foliage has been, oh, so much more than a lawn on the lip, sir. 'Tis what we are, and why we are it. And when everyone else got out of the pirate business, The Stache stuck it out, knowing one day my ship would come in. This is the day. This is the ship. *(menacingly)* Now, cough up that key, my Lord.

Aster Not a chance, you thug.

> *STACHE throws a tantrum at this insult, then recovers.*

Stache *(to SMEE)* Why, is that my Lord's coat you're holding?

> *SMEE helps STACHE on with Aster's coat.*

Smee Looks to be about your size, Cap'n.

Stache What the well-dressed "thug" is wearing this season.

Smee So *comme il faut*, Cap'n. So very *comme il faut*.

> *STACHE surveys his reflection in a mirror. He's pleased with what he sees.*

Stache I say, Smee – what is it the men call me?

Smee Nancy, sir?

Stache No, the other thing.

Smee Ruthless, sir. Ruthless, Heartless, and Peerless.

Stache *(so sweetly)* Guilty as charged. *(to ASTER)* Now, give us the key!

Aster Never.

Stache Playing games is for children, Lord Aster, and I hate, I hate, I hate children! *(hurls his bucket at the mirror, smashing it)* Bring it in, Gómez!

Sánchez It's Sánchez, sir.

Stache *(so hard to find good help these days)* Just . . . bring it in. Thanks ever so. *(PIRATES drag in the* *trunk.)* The *Wasp* is my ship now, and everything aboard her belongs to me, including the treasure Victoria thinks nobody knows about. Silly old queen.

Aster God Save Her.

Stache Queen.

Aster God Save Her.

Stache Victoria.

Aster God Save Her.

Stache Banana.

Aster God Save –

Stache *(gotcha!)* Oopsy! *(The PIRATES appreciate ASTER's humiliation. STACHE perches on the trunk.)* Here's two things. When I open this swag, I'll be the single most significant pirate in the world, the solar system, or other places yet to be discovered anywhere in the universe.

　　　　A moment passes.

Aster That's only one thing –

Stache The second thing is a dilemma, a large one, the Cadillac Escalade of dilemmas, in point of fact – for a little bird tells me that your darling daughter is sailing to Rundoon on the safer southern route, aboard the *Navel Nerd.*

Smee The *Neverland*, sir.

Stache Huh?

Smee The *Neverland*, sir.

Stache Same letters: *Navel Nerd – Neverland.* I was close. I was pretty darn close! Splitting rabbits, really . . .

Smee Hairs, sir.

Stache Splitting hares, that too. *(to ASTER, cheerfully)* Oh! OH! Just a sec! I know you love your Molly above rubies. What say you to a quick detour, we pluck her off the *Neverland*, and you can watch her die! Unless you're feeling a weensy bit more amenable? *(eyes ASTER, whose hand gives him away)* Love yer locket! But what's in yer pocket? Oh, allow me! *(reaches in and extracts the key)* Done 'n' dusted, kippers 'n' custard. Here's the key, boys!

> *The PIRATES are so focused on the key, they don't notice that the amulet around Aster's neck begins to glow. There is a sound of bells. Freeze.*

SCENE SIX

The Neverland—*Passageway*

> *Molly's matching amulet begins to glow as well. Bells ring.*

Molly *(holding the amulet)* My father. He's in trouble.

Prentiss Your neck-thing is glowing.

Ted And ringing.

Molly Don't ask me about that.

Prentiss I can ask whatever I want. I'm the leader.

Boy Lay off, Prentiss. *(to MOLLY)* C'mon, you have to tell.

Molly All right, listen. *(furtively)* My father is going to Rundoon on a secret mission for the Queen.

Boy What's a mission?

Mrs. Bumbrake *(from off)* Molly! Where are you, girl?

> *MOLLY bundles the BOYS down another corridor.*

Molly Ssssh! Down this gangway, and keep it quiet!

Ted Tell me again, what was it called, what we ate?

Molly   Pork chops, pork salad, and pork belly pie.

Ted   Greatest night of my life.

Molly   Sssshhh! There's more tomorrow if we don't get caught.

Ted   "Pork" – beautiful word.

>   *A different, louder bell is heard outside Slank's cabin.*

Boy   There's the ringing again –

Prentiss   Her neck-thing –

Molly   No, it's coming from someplace else.

>   *The shadow of a cat appears on Slank's cabin door, a glow emanating from within.*

Boy   Behind this door.

Molly   Get away, Boy! Don't open that cabin!

>   *The BOY opens it anyway. The horrible ship's cat flies gently out, floating, lighter than air, gurgling and cooing sweetly.*

Boy   Holy – !

Molly   Slank's – !

Ted   Cat – !

Prentiss   Flying!

Narrator Stache   We ask you now to imagine a grown cat in flight –

Narrator Slank   – suspended in space as if hanging from a string.

Narrator Smee   Of course, the boys don't have to imagine –

Narrator Alf   – because there they are, and there's the cat –

Narrator Bumbrake   – and that cat is definitely flying –

Narrator Scott   – and those bells are definitely ringing –

Narrator Aster – and that cabin is definitely glowing.

Molly Glowing – ringing – flying – it can only mean one thing!

Aster *(holding his amulet)* Starstuff!

Molly Starstuff! The Queen's trunk is in Slank's cabin! *(slams the cabin door shut, grunting from the effort and extinguishing the glow and bells)* Okay, nothing to see here, move along.

Ted But that cat was –

Molly No it wasn't.

Prentiss Yes it was! Tubby's right! Your neck-thing was ringing and Slank's cat was totally fly –

Molly *(distracting them from the flying cat)* Hey – y'know what'd be fun? Howzabout a bedtime story!

Ted What's that?

Molly Oh, ha-ha, very amus – *(realizing)* omigosh – you poor things. You've never had a bedtime story?

Prentiss This might sound kinda defensive –

Ted Hard to have a bedtime when you don't have a bed.

Molly Sorry. Sorry, I didn't mean to –

Boy Tell you what. You say "sorry" so easy, like the rough patch's smoothed over, no hard feelings and everything's fixed. Well, no. There's dark . . . a mass of darkness in the world, and if you get trapped in that cave like us, it beats you down. "Sorry" can't fix it. Better to say nothing than "sorry." *(hearing his mother's song, far away)* When it's night, and I'm too scared to sleep, I look through the cracks, y'know? – between the wood nailed over the window – and I see all those little stars that I can't reach, and I think that in a hundred years, or two or three hundred maybe, boys'll be free and life'll be so beautiful that nobody'll ever say "sorry" again – 'cuz nobody'll have to. I think about that a lot.

MOLLY is moved by this glimpse into the boy's soul. So are TED and PRENTISS.

Prentiss Well, that's more than he said in the last thirteen years.

Boy So, bedtime stories? Not a big priority, okay?

Molly No, it's not okay. I'm giving you one. It's a gift. Least I can do. Like, um – *Sleeping Beauty. Sleeping Beauty*'s a good one. You'll like it. There's a kiss in it. True Love's Kiss.

Ted Yeah! *(then)* I don't know what that is.

Molly Then I'll tell you. C'mon – back to your cabin and I'll be Mother. Now – the story of Sleeping Beauty. "Once upon a time" – that's how they always start – "Once upon a time, a beautiful baby was born . . ."

MOLLY, Pied Piper-like, lures the BOYS off.

SCENE SEVEN

The Wasp—*Captain's Cabin*

STACHE enters, finishing his own fairy tale.

Stache " . . . and that beautiful baby had a big, bushy handlebar, and *it* grew out as he grew *up* and they both lived awfully ever after. The end." *(rises, exultant, key in hand)* From this day forth, it'll be nothing but pleasure cruises and the odd America's Cup for me. Now, open – *(unlocks the trunk and throws open the lid)* and perpend! *(A Piratical Silence of Great Awfulness.)* What is that?

Smee It's sand, sir.

31

Aster Sand? But that's impossible.

Stache When you say sand, do you mean the utterly worthless granular material one associates with the water's edge?

Smee Yes, sir.

Stache I see. *(then, to ASTER)* Perchance you think a treasure trunk *sans* treasure has put my piratical BVDs in a twist? How wrong you are. Yes, I'd hoped to be hip-deep in diamonds, but they're a poor substitute for what I really crave: a bona fide hero to help me feel whole. For without a hero, what am I? Half a villain; a pirate in part; ruthless, but toothless. And then I saw *you*, and I thought, "Maybe? Can it be? Is he the one I've waited for? Would he, for example, give up something precious for the daughter he loves?" But alas, he gives up sand. Now, let's see. Hero with treasure, very good. Hero with no treasure . . . doable. No hero and a trunk full o' sand? Not so much. *(suddenly monstrous)* NOW, WHERE'S MY TREASURE?!?

Smee What if they swapped the trunks, sir?

Stache Swapped, y'say?

Smee *(smacks himself on the head)* Stupid idea, Smee. Stupid, stupid!

Stache Swapped, yes. Switched – right there on the dike.

Smee Deck.

Stache Deck. In which case –

Smee The trunk with the treasure's aboard the *Neverland*.

Stache Destiny check! What do we know about the *Neverland*?

Smee She's a slow ship, Cap'n.

Stache Sadly slow. And what of our ship, the *Wasp*?

Smee We're fast, Cap'n.

Stache   Superfast! Which means we're leagues ahead of her by now, Einstein! Change of course! *(to SÁNCHEZ)* Hard about! *(turns on ASTER)* You're behind this swappery, Aster, or I'm the Queen of England!

Aster   God Save Her.

Stache   Oh shut up! *(to SÁNCHEZ)* I said hard about, Gómez!

Sánchez   It's Sánchez, sir.

Stache   Hit the pedal, Gretel!

Sánchez   That's Sánchez, sir!

Stache   Burn rubber, Bubba!

Sánchez   *¡Ay de mi! ¡Qué demonio! ¡Debo protestar!*

Stache   GIVE ME IT, Y'SHROOM! *(takes control of wheel)* You pay peanuts, you get monkeys. Now, juice it! The chase is on! The die is cast! The game's afoot – ! *(jumps on trunk but trips and crashes; quickly recovers and strikes a majestic reclining pose)* I want that treasure, boys! Catch me a *Neverland*!!

  STACHE is carried off atop the trunk, to victory.

SCENE EIGHT

The Neverland—*Bilge Dungeon*

With the BOYS curled at her feet, MOLLY finishes her bedtime story.

Molly   And, as the Princess slept, a thick forest grew up around the castle, keeping everybody out. Everybody but one man. Boys?

Boy   *(nearly asleep)* The Prince, right?

Molly The Prince, yes, very good. He chopped his way to Sleeping Beauty's room, saw his true love and kissed her, just once, sweetly on the lips.

Ted *(in his sleep)* Mmm . . . pork.

Molly And True Love's Kiss broke the spell, the Princess found her Prince, and they all lived happily ever – *(Her amulet suddenly glows and rings.)* The amulet again! Talk to me, Daddy!

> *MOLLY leaves the sleeping boys and heads for the deck. ASTER appears on the* Wasp.

Narrator Aster With the *Wasp* racing at flank speed for the *Neverland*, Leonard Aster clears his mind and tries to reach Molly.

> *They lift their amulets away from their chests for better reception.*

Molly Daddy, are you there? Hello, hello?

Aster Can you hear me now? *(adjusts amulet)* Can you hear me now?

Molly Daddy – the Queen's trunk is here, on board the *Neverland*!

Aster Not in English! Too dangerous.

Molly Oh dear, please don't speak in –

Aster *(ad libs) Brump burp wheee!*

Molly Oh Daddy, not Dodo.

Aster *Myah myah vrrreeep!*

Molly Parrots? A flock of parrots?

Aster *Vrrrraaap, vrrrrreeep! Eeeep!*

Molly Parrots have taken over your ship? Well, what genius brought parrots – ?

Aster PIRATES! We've been taken over by pirates!

Molly Pirates! Oh, that hard "i" sound is so tricky –

Aster MOLLY! The *Wasp* is bearing down on the

Neverland! Soon as we catch you, steer clear of Black Stache and BRING THE TRUNK TO ME!

Molly I will!

Aster Don't let me down, Daughter! This is your mission now!

Molly *(ecstatic at the responsibility)* Yes, sir. Thank you, sir! *Cwa-cwah! Cwa-cwah! Vreeeep!*

> *The BOY appears.*

Boy What are you doing?

> *Startled, MOLLY lets go of her amulet. Lights out on ASTER.*

SCENE NINE

The Neverland—*On Deck*

> *MOLLY turns to find the BOY on the deck behind her.*

Molly Sorry, what? Um – get below, boy. If Slank sees you on deck, he'll rear up like the –

Boy You were talking to your neck-thing.

Molly No, I wasn't.

Boy I know what I saw.

Molly Well, there was . . . there was a porpoise swimming alongside the ship, and it was making those funny noises that porpoises make, and I thought I'd make some funny noises too, that's all.

Boy So you were talking to a fish.

Molly Porpoises are not fish. They're mammals, just like you. Or Germans.

Boy Then how come your neck-thing glows and rings all by itself?

Molly *(not very convincing)* It's for swimming. I'm a good swimmer. It's a swimming medal.

Boy Right. Swimming. Sure. And what's starstuff?

Molly Decision. I'm going to trust you.

Boy Why? I'm just a boy.

Molly I know. Pity. *(remembers the boy's "sorry" manifesto, looks at the sky)* You like to look at the stars? Well, there they are –

Boy There's so many . . .

Molly They look safe, don't they, sparkling up there like diamonds.

Boy I like when they shoot across the sky! *Shooom!*

Molly *(suddenly very like her father)* Sometimes pieces of them fall to earth – little bits that look like sand. Can you keep a secret?

Boy I can.

All WE CAN.

Molly Those little bits are starstuff. The trunk in Slank's cabin is full of it. *(grabs her amulet)* There's some in here too, in case I'm ever in trouble.

Boy *(tries to touch the amulet)* Starstuff?? Lemme see!!

Molly NO!! *(pulls the amulet away)* It changes people if they touch it.

Boy How?

Molly Different ways – depending on what they want to be.

Boy So if somebody gets their hands on this starstuff and –

Molly – and they're evil and greedy like Genghis Khan, or they're hungry for world domination like Caesar or Napoleon or, you know, Ayn Rand –

Boy Who's that?

Molly Uch, didn't you learn anything at that orphanage?

Boy Was kinda busy trying not to die.

Molly Oh.

Boy So if starstuff's so dangerous, why're you after it?

Molly I'm a Starcatcher. We have special powers that we
use in secret – to keep starstuff away from tyrants who
try to rule the world.

Boy You mean, like Queen Victoria?

Molly God Save Her. And no, that's different. She doesn't
need starstuff to rule the world. She's British.

Boy So you're a – what is it?

Molly Starcatcher. There's only six and a half of us on
the planet.

Boy Six and a half?

Molly I'm still an apprentice.

Boy Okay, so prove it.

Molly What?

Boy Go on, amaze me with your special powers.

Molly It's not a magic show. I'm not like some magician
guy.

Boy Well, I mean if you can't actually do anything . . .

Molly Fine, whatever. *(then)* To have faith is to have
wings.

> *MOLLY clasps the amulet tightly, closes her eyes,
> and floats a few inches off the deck . . . then down
> again.*

Boy Whoa.

Molly Satisfied?

Boy So the cat was flying. C'mon, I wanna fly, too! Like
you and the cat!

Molly Get serious, will you?! The starstuff has to be
destroyed.

Boy *(not believing in himself yet)* You want me to destroy it??

Molly Don't be ridiculous. My father is going to throw it into the world's hottest active volcano – Mount Jalapeño.

Boy Where's that?

Molly Rundoon, wouldn't you know it. Problem is, King Zarboff would kill for even a thimble of starstuff!

Boy Hey, I can help. See, I'm gonna be the king's new helper. So when we get to Rundoon, I'll just ask him –

Molly You're not going to be his helper. You're going to be snake food! Zarboff likes to buy orphans and feed them to his snakes!

Boy So Grempkin lied.

Molly King Zarboff the Third is evil – he's the worst Zarboff yet!

Boy Grown-ups always lie! It's all they ever do!

Molly You want to help? Then help me get that trunk to my father!

Boy Hey, you know what? Forget it! Why should I help anybody?? WHAT'S ANYBODY EVER DONE FOR ME??

Out of nowhere, SLANK!

Slank You!

Boy *(furious)* Snake food? Really?

Slank *(circling the BOY like a shark about to attack)* I told you to stay in yer crate, orphan sludge.

Boy When exactly were you gonna tell us we were –

Slank That's it. Bill Slank is drawin' the line! I may not have been born with a silver spoon up me bum, but that don't mean I won't stir my tea with one!

Molly   Ew.

Boy   That's gross.

Molly   Get below, boy!

> *MOLLY gets safely out of harm's way, but SLANK brutally hurls his whip and snags the BOY.*

Slank   He ain't goin' below, he's goin' over!

Boy   Let go! Lemme go!

> *SLANK reels the BOY in, close to the rail of the ship. The* Neverland *is lurching now, the sea below churning and getting wilder.*

Slank   Zarboff promised me his whole bleedin' fleet in exchange for the trunk in my cabin.

Narrator Alf   Strong gusts blowing, winds hit 34 knots!

Boy   *(fighting for his life)* I HATE GROWN-UPS!

Slank   Make like a kitten – take a long, long time to drown! Bottom's up, boy!

> *SLANK lifts the BOY overhead, holding him perilously aloft.*

Boy   Not overboard! Please! I can't –

Slank   Can't what?

Boy   SWIM!

> *SLANK tosses the BOY into the sea. He sinks below the waves, then claws his way to the surface, spitting up water. MOLLY swims on.*

Molly   Here I am, boy! All will be well!

> *MOLLY saves the BOY and backstrokes him to the ship and safety. A gull flies over the waves, squawking at the rising storm and the roiling sea.*

SCENE TEN

The Neverland *and The* Wasp

Narrator Scott Winds approaching 40 knots, whitecaps heavy, crests overhanging!

> *On the* Neverland, *a SAILOR spots the* Wasp *on the horizon and yells down to the deck below.*

Sailor Smee Ship off the forward bow! From the cut of 'er jib, she could be the *Wasp*!

Sailor Scott The *Wasp*? After us? Better tell Slank!

> *Thunder! MOLLY drags the BOY on and drops him with a thud.*

Molly Backstroke is my event, and I do so like to finish first. I win more medals at school than anyone, except for Daphne Cooper – but Daphne Cooper's a swot. *(kicks the BOY in the side)* Deep breaths. There we go.

Boy *(spits and coughs, then)* You saved my life.

Molly Of course.

Boy Why?

Molly Because I'm the leader.

Boy But you don't even like me.

Molly The leader can't go about saving only the people she likes.

Boy The leader has to be a boy.

Molly Only if the boy knows there's more important things in this world than saving his own neck.

Boy Like what?

Molly Like saving someone else's.

Slank *(from amidships)* They figgered out I swapped the trunks!

Boy Slank!

Molly We need the *Wasp* to catch up to us quick!

MOLLY runs off. SLANK enters, leaves the wheel to MACK, and looks out to sea. The BOY hides, within hearing distance.

Slank It's the *Wasp* all right! Sally Lunn, she's a fast ship!

Mack We'll never outrun a frigate, Captain.

Slank We can bleedin' well try! *(barks an order)* Billow the wopsil! *(The* Neverland *begins to sway and creak.)* Here's the breeze now, ye bilge-rats! *(to the* Wasp*)* Y'want yer trunk, Leonard Aster? You'll have to catch me first! *(to MACK)* Follow the wind, weevil! Hard to starboard!

Mack *(comes down to SLANK, holding up his branded hand)* Starboard? That ain't the one with the big P, is it?

Slank BRING ME THE BRANDING IRON!

The BOY runs to the wheel and spins it furiously.

Narrator Boy The boy spins the ship's wheel for everything he's worth!

The Neverland *bucks!*

Slank He's changed our course!

Boy, Slank, Mack STRAIGHT FOR THE *WASP*!

Triumphant, the BOY spins the wheel wildly.

Narrators Stache, Molly Wind 47 knots!

Narrators GALE WARNING!

Narrators Prentiss, Ted The ship's wheel careens across the deck and spins out to sea –

Narrators Scott, Smee – turning the *Neverland* hard against the grain –

Narrator Smee – and jolting two people in a tiny cabin below!

ALF and MRS. BUMBRAKE, in her tiny cabin.

Alf, Mrs. Bumbrake *(singing)*
I'VE WAITED FOR LOVE,
I'VE WAITED FOR BLISS,
I'VE WAITED FOR THIS –

ALF is about to kiss MRS. BUMBRAKE, but she pushes him away –

Mrs. Bumbrake No! No more nattering. I'm still a Nana and I must find Molly. *(JOLT! They stagger.)* Spit me over, what was that?!

Alf We're changing course is all – straight for the Isle of Love –

Mrs. Bumbrake But where's my Molly? *(ALF begins kissing up her arm.)* She's been lost ever so long. *(Kiss kiss kiss.)* Cease and desist, sir! *(suddenly stands up with a manly voice)* HEY!! Cut the canoodling! I gotta grab the girl, get it!?! *(instantly all flirty again)* But do come with.

ALF, MRS. BUMBRAKE, and the cabin are gone.

Narrators Aster, Ted, Boy, Scott Wind 55 knots! Strong gale, rolling seas, blowing spray!

Narrators Prentiss, Ted, Molly The *Neverland* crashes into the waves!

Narrators Stache, Smee Bucking and barreling straight for the *Wasp*!

STACHE stands at the bow of the Wasp, *his PIRATES crouching around the mast.*

Act One: Scene Ten

Stache Sweeten the choppers 'n' reef the expedient. This wind'll throw guano something fierce in yer face! Oi! D'you see what I see, Smee?

Smee The *Neverland*, Cap'n! She's headin' right for us!

Stache This is too easy! I think I'm even feeling a weensy bit guilty. *(pouts a moment)* And . . . I'm over it. *(barks the command)* Up the gunter! Prepare to board!

Smee Up the gunter!

> *The PIRATES buck with a huge, rolling wave!*

Stache And keep the Union Jack flying so Bill Slank thinks we'll be polite!

Smee So devious! So very devious!

Stache *Neverland*, HO! Victory is OURS! Well, MINE!

Narrators WIND 63 KNOTS: HURRICANO! VIOLENT STORM! VISIBILITY GONE! WHOLE WAVES! BLACK SKIES! RED OVER WHITE OVER RED!

> *On the deck of the* Neverland, *looking up at the* Wasp:

Slank Pucker up, lads! We'll kiss her any minute now!

Sailor Scott But she's one of ours! We'll be ramming a British ship!!

Mack The damn'd orphan boy – he's ruined us!

Slank Orphans ruin everything! Hold on to yer ditty bag, boys! Here comes the *Wasp*!

Narrator Mack Two ships make toward each other, tiny craft against the bounding main.

> *A long shot of the open sea. TWO CREWS assemble behind two captains, steering two tiny ships and two similar trunks toward a moment of reckoning. STACHE and his PIRATES, with the sand trunk on the* Wasp, *behave like British twits.*

43

Stache Lordy, lordy – just in time for tea.

Pirate Bumbrake Scones from Fortnum's!

Pirate Aster Devon cream!

Slank *(on the* Neverland*)* We can beat her, boys! She's only a ship full o' fops!

Smee *(on the* Wasp*)* Now, Boss?

Stache Now! Run up the Jolly Roger!

> *A PIRATE replaces the Union Jack with the pirate flag. The PIRATES abandon their foppishness and turn instantly vicious.*

Slank It's pirates! *(to fleeing SAILORS)* Come back, ye cowards!!

> *But it's too late. STACHE stands on the deck of the* Neverland, *behind him a phalanx of PIRATES.*

Stache Hallo, *Neverland.* I believe this trunk belongs to you. And you have something of ours.

> *Melee! Then, freeze!*

Slank *(to himself, edging away)* Save yer trunk, Bill. Get the trunk to Zarboff and you'll be too posh to push!

> *Melee! Then, freeze!*

Narrator Prentiss Wind 67 knots! That's 200 miles – *(suddenly self-conscious)* Everybody!

Narrators THAT'S 200 MILES PER HOUR! LARGE WAVES OVER 50 FEET! DISASTER! DESTRUC-TION! DEVASTATION!

> *MOLLY finds the BOYS below deck in the bilge dungeon.*

Molly You! Boy! You turned us around so the *Wasp* could catch us!

44

Boy Pretty cheeky, huh?

Molly *(delighted by this fellow)* Pretty cheeky.

Prentiss Yeah, awesome – and now there's pirates everywhere! Good move, ace.

Molly He did something big, Prentiss.

Boy I could do more.

Prentiss Well, I'm still the leader.

Molly Then help me get the trunk out of Slank's cabin and onto the *Wasp*!

Prentiss Sorry, not our issue.

Molly Never mind, I'll do it myself. Mrs. Bumbrake! Mrs. Bumbrake!

> *MOLLY runs out. The door slams.*

Ted *(to the BOY)* You're different, you know that? *(to PRENTISS)* Don't you think he's different?

Prentiss We should definitely wait here. We'll be safer.

Boy There's more important things in this world than saving your own neck.

Prentiss, Ted Like what?

Boy Like helping Molly.

> *The BOY runs off. A boxing bell rings: DING, DING, DING!*

Narrator Scott And, up on deck, two captains square off for the greatest of grand prizes!

> *A boxing ring forms around SLANK and STACHE.*

Boxing Announcer Prentiss Ladies and gentlemen, thanks for coming out on this stormy night for our featured bout! In this corner, direct from Slough by way of Despond, with the intimacy issues and the claggy knickers, it's no mother's son and no man's pal: BILL "THE RAT BASTARD" SLANK! *(ALL cheer.)* And in this corner, sporting his famous flavor-saver since the

45

tender age of ten, the most fearsome pirate on the pike, all hands on deck for THE BLACK STACHE! *(SMEE, alone, cheers STACHE.)* This is a one-round knockout match. Kicking, spitting, and gouging is preferred. Hitting below the belt is not required, though the fans tend to like it.

All WE LOVE IT!!

Boxing Announcer Prentiss Now shake hands and come out rhyming!

> *A (s)word fight between SLANK and STACHE.*

Slank Take a hike, y'mingy crumb! The trunk is mine, so kiss me bum!

Stache I'll kiss ya, Bill, with me French-roaster, rolley-coaster, upper-cutter flipper-flopper!

Slank Which I dodge like so, behind-your-backsie, which needs-a-waxy, by the by!

Stache Or me God's-anointed, double-jointed, triple-pointed belly-whopper!

Slank Or me on-yer-kneesy, easy-peasy, Java-neesy battle-cry!

Stache Me dog's dinner!

Slank Me shark-shanker!

Stache Me winkle-pinner!

Slank Me walk-the-planker!

Stache "Shall I compare thee to a summer's day?" *(cold-cocks SLANK)* There he lies – a jumped-up cabin boy who doesn't know his place. *(approaching SLANK lethally)* Gimme the Queen's trunk or say yer g'byes, y' bathtub captain!

> *STACHE raises his weapon. But – CRACK!!!*
> *Lightning strikes the Neverland. EVERYONE*
> *scatters. MOLLY, atop the Queen's trunk, hurtles*

across the deck, howling. STACHE and SLANK reenter.

Narrator Stache CRACK! The sound of splintering wood! Flapping canvas whipped by wind!

Narrator Slank CRACK! The deck is breaking up! Mast that was, a mast no more!

Narrator Stache The *Neverland* –

Narrator Slank – she's split in two!

Narrator Stache Stem to stern!

Narrator Slank Fore and aft!

Narrators A WHOLE SHIP HALF'D!!

Two SAILORS split a model of the Neverland *in two. The COMPANY splits and tumbles, half of the company with each half of the ship, the churning sea in between.*

Sailor Boy Abandon ship! Abandon ship!

Sailor Smee She's broke in half! Main-brace's gone!

MOLLY and MRS. BUMBRAKE struggle with the Queen's trunk.

Molly We're saving the trunk, and that's all there is to it!

SLANK appears out of nowhere.

Slank Oi! You really missed the gravy boat, Betty – you and yer sea green eyes.

Mrs. Bumbrake Don't let him smell your fear, Molly! *(to SLANK, outraged on behalf of her eye color)* And they're hazel! *(calling off urgently)* ALF, LEND A HAND!

Slank *(pushing MOLLY aside)* Outta my way! *(grabbing the trunk)* ALL I WANT'S ME TRUNK!!

SLANK and MRS. BUMBRAKE battle for the trunk. ALF enters and stands up to the boss.

47

Alf   Don't ye touch one hair on that woman's legs!

Slank   She's all yours, lover boy!

Alf   NOW, BETTY!

> *MRS. BUMBRAKE grabs the ship's cat and throws the screeching animal in SLANK's face.*

Narrator Alf   Slank gets his cat right in the puss!

> *ALF tosses SLANK and the cat overboard.*

Alf   Down ye go to dinner!

Narrator Mack   But just before bunking with Davy Jones –

Slank   *(in a watery close-up)* O, the waves swallow me up, a great shroud of sea. And the sharks start nibbling away, like me mother's kisses – MOTHER! Ye left me on the steps of a tattoo parlor, wrapped in a half-eaten bag of fish 'n' chips. Round me neck, a note: "Orphan Bill Slank – Too wicked to end well."

> *The waves cover SLANK forever.*

Narrator Mack   TTFN!

Alf   *(hollering overboard)* Ye good fer nothing bucket o' scum!

Mrs. Bumbrake   My white knight!!

Molly   Now, let's get moving!

> *ASTER appears on the* Wasp, *holding his amulet, telepathing.*

Aster   Molly! Molly, I'm locked in the broom cabin!

Molly   *(holds her amulet, triumphant)* DADDY, THE TRUNK IS OURS!

Aster   BRING IT TO ME!!

> *On the other half of the* Neverland.

Pirate Slank   Abandon ship!

Pirate Alf   Abandon ship!

SMEE enters with the trunk full of sand.

Smee *(airport-style announcement)* Check your trunks! Some trunks may appear identical to other trunks!

Pirate Alf *(running past SMEE)* Save yerself!

> *SMEE runs off. The BOY runs on. MOLLY, atop the Queen's trunk on the other half of the* Neverland, *spots him.*

Molly Help, Boy! I need more time to get the Queen's trunk to my father!

Boy *(sees the sand trunk just sitting there)* Don't worry! I'll stall the pirates! *(sits on the trunk, all innocence, as STACHE runs past)* Some crazy weather, huh?

Stache *(stops dead, spins)* What are you?

Boy What are you?

Stache WHAT AM I?!?

Pirates BLACK STACHE!!!

Boy Never heard o' you.

Stache Liar! The Stache is on everyone's lips. *(nonchalantly)* Why, is that the Queen's trunk you're sitting on?

Boy Oh yeah, Queen's trunk, totally. Molly Aster told me to protect it.

Stache From who?

Boy Pirates like you.

Stache But we have all the fun!

Boy You do?

Stache Abso-loony. A little swash, a bit o' buckle – you'd love it more than bread! Now, give us the trunk and join the party . . . er . . . appellation, please. *(off the BOY's blank face)* Yer name, bub.

Boy No name. Orphan.

Stache *(affecting pity)* You're more at sea than Columbus, boy. If you were a pirate, you'd have a proper name.

Boy You could do that?

Stache I'm the boss, ain't I? How about Bluebeard Bob? *(nixes this)* Long John Larry? *(a thought)* Oooh! We hung a bloke from the yardarm week ago Wednesday – Pirate Pete. That's available.

Boy Pirate Pete . . .

Stache Good solid name is Peter, like a rock. That's what you'll be, boy, my rock. Now, gimme the trunk.

Boy *(hereafter called PETER)* Peter. Yeah. I like that.

Stache Iconic as the moonwalk in a Michael Jackson video. Now, gimme the trunk.

Peter And what would I do?

Stache You'd star in my nasty crew. Infamy! Calamity! Fraternity! You need to connect, boy.

Peter Peter.

Stache You need to connect, Peter. No man is an archipelago. Now, be a good Peter and give your captain his GREAT BIG TREASURE!! *(throws PETER off the trunk and flings it open!)* Sand again!

Peter You blew it, Stache! The Queen's trunk's safe on the *Wasp!* *(calling off)* We saved the treasure, Molly!! We saved the world!!!

Stache You're killing my buzz, boy – to which I say die!

STACHE throws PETER overboard.

Peter Not again!

PETER falls into the sea and bobs on one side of the stage. Across, ASTER appears on the Wasp. *In between, MOLLY stands on the Queen's trunk aboard what's left of the* Neverland.

Molly Not again! The boy's gone overboard!!

Aster Molly, bring me the trunk!

Peter Help! I can't swim!

Molly But Daddy, the boy needs help!

Aster Molly, this is a direct order! BRING THE TRUNK TO ME!

Molly This trunk floats, boy!

Peter My name's Peter!

Molly Peter! I like it!

Peter Me too!

Molly There's an island, Peter! Ride the trunk to the island!

> *MOLLY pushes the Queen's trunk overboard.*

Aster Molly, no!!!

> *Tempest-tossed by the terrible storm, everyone prepares to abandon ship.*

All *(singing)*
CRACK AND RIP AND CRACK AGAIN!
SOAKED BY SEA AND SOAKED BY RAIN!
SOON, WE PRAY, THE STORM BE DONE,
AND WHEN IT'S DONE,
PRAY YOU SEE THE SUN!

> *From out of the sea-spray, ALF clings to MRS. BUMBRAKE.*

Alf
GRAB A SPAR, MRS. BUMBRAKE, GRAB A SPAR!
Mrs. Bumbrake
WHAT'S A SPAR?
Alf
THIS IS NO TIME TO ARGUE,
AND WE CAN'T STAY WHERE WE ARE!

Mrs. Bumbrake

OH, THE WIND IS LIKE A WHIP!

Alf

TAKE ME HAND! ABANDON SHIP!

Mrs. Bumbrake

BUT MY MOLLY, OH MY MOLLY –
WHAT A BLOODY AWFUL TRIP!

> *ALF and MRS. BUMBRAKE jump! STACHE and*
> *SMEE appear, railing against the storm.*

Stache

BLOW YOU WINDS! OH, YOU WINDS!
I'M STILL THE MAN!

Smee

YOU'RE THE MAN!

Stache

THANK YOU, SMEE. CARRY ME
AND ALL THE OTHER CRAP YOU CAN!
EVEN IN THE CHURNING SEA,
STILL AM I THE CAPTAIN, SMEE.
AND THE PIRATE CODE I FOLLOW:
"ONE FOR ALL, AND ALL FOR ME!"

> *STACHE and SMEE jump!*

Prentiss

I'M THE LEADER!

Ted

NO, YOU'RE NOT!

Prentiss

YES I AM!

Ted

WHEN THERE'S A FEW OF US.
THERE CAN'T BE A LEADER NOW!

Prentiss
WHY NOT?
Ted
THERE'S ONLY TWO OF US!
Prentiss
JUMP! C'MON TED! WE'LL JUMP TOGETHER!
Ted
I WAS THINKING WE COULD MAYBE
WAIT FOR SLIGHTLY BETTER WEATHER!

> *PRENTISS and TED jump! MOLLY appears,*
> *preparing to dive into the sea.*

All *(except Molly)*
THE NEVERLAND *HAS COME APART!*
SCREW YOUR COURAGE, STEEL YOUR HEART!
Molly
SOMEWHERE OUT THERE, SEARCH FOR HIM!
DIVE, MOLLY ASTER, AND SWIM!
All
SWIM ON AGAINST THE CURRENT.
SWIM ON AGAINST THE SEA,
THO' THE TIDE MAY TURN AGAINST US,
THO' TOO STRONG THE TIDE MAY BE.
THO' EACH STROKE, EACH STROKE GROWS HEAVY,
THO' EACH BREATH IS AGONY,
WE TRY, 'TIL WE CAN BREATHE NO MORE.
TO CLAMBER UP THE NEAREST SHORE,
AND FALL UPON OUR KNEES BEFORE
THE TRUTH THAT SETS US FREE –

> *PETER floats atop the Queen's trunk, fashioning a*
> *mast from a branch. He pulls off his shirt and drapes*
> *it on the branch, making a sail. It catches the wind*
> *and PETER is blown toward the island.*

Stache Follow that trunk, Smee! Get me to that island!

Molly Get to the island, Peter! And don't let that trunk out of your sight!!

> *The clouds lift, and the low, setting sun breaks through.*

All

> *SWIM ON AGAINST THE CURRENT.*
> *SWIM ON AGAINST THE SEA,*
> *THO' THE TIDE MAY TURN AGAINST YOU,*
> *THO' TOO STRONG THE TIDE MAY BE.*
> *AND THO' YOUR ARMS BE LEADEN*
> *SLICING THROUGH THE SPRAY AND FOAM,*
> *SWIM ON, SWIM ON,*
> *SWIM ON, SWIM ON.*
> *SWIM ON AGAINST THE CURRENT*
> *'TIL YOUR COURAGE BRINGS YOU HOME,*
> *'TIL YOU STAND*
> *ON THE LAND*
> *SAFELY HOME!*

> *PETER, now jubilant atop the trunk, sails toward the green island. BLACKOUT.*

END OF ACT ONE.

Act Two

PROLOGUE

Mollusk Island—Shore

*A fetching mob of MERMAIDS enters in front of the
curtain to celebrate their encounter with starstuff.*

Mermaid Stache   *(singing)*

   YOU'RE LIKELY WOND'RING
   WHAT WE'VE HAD TO DRINK NOW.
   AND YOU MIGHT THINK, "NOW,
   THEY'VE GONE TOO FAR."
   BUT SOMETHING WE SHOULD
   NOT HAVE BEEN EXPOSED TO
   WE GOT TOO CLOSE TO
   BY SWIMMING AFT
   OF PETER'S RAFT,
   AND HERE WE ARE.
   AND IT WAS STARSTUFF
   FROM THE SKIES
   THAT MADE EACH FISH
   THE LOVELY DISH
   BEFORE YOUR EYES.
   NOW FINS ARE FINGERS,

55

HUMAN-STYLE.
BECAUSE OF STARSTUFF
WE SMILE.

All

AND IT WAS STARSTUFF
FROM ABOVE.

Mermaid Stache

IT GAVE US NECKS.
IT GAVE US PECS.
WHAT'S NOT TO LOVE?

All

OH, HOW WE TINGLE,
AND EV'RY DAY'S SPRING.
BECAUSE OF STARSTUFF
WE SING.
OH YES, IT'S STARSTUFF

Mermaid Alf

I WAS A FLOUNDER, YESSIR!

All

WE ADORE.

Mermaid Ted

AND I, A SMELT.

All

I GOT A BUZZ.
OH, WHAT IT DOES!
I WANT SOME MORE!

Mermaid Molly

I WAS A YELLOWTAIL TUNA 'TIL I FELT

All

I'M ALL WARM AND FUZZY

Mermaid Molly

A WARM AND FUZZY FEELING –

All

I'M WILD AND FREE!

Mermaid Molly

MY FINGERS TINGLED
AND MY HEART STARTED REELING –

All

I LOVE HOW STARSTUFF
(MM-MM)

Mermaid Molly

'TIL STARSTUFF MADE MY TUNA MELT!

All

IT MADE A MERMAID OUTTA ME!
IT WAS THE STARSTUFF

Mermaid Scott

AND OH WHAT A GLOW
AS YOUR FINS START A-GROWING SOME MORE.

All

THAT DISSOLVED.

Mermaid Smee

GO WITH THE FLOW
AS THE GLOW GETS YA GOIN' SOME MORE.

All

YOU GET A THRILL,

Mermaid Alf

SOON YOU'RE BREATHIN' AIR.

All

YOU LOSE A GILL,

Mermaid Stache

SOON YOU'RE GROWING HAIR.

All

YOUR PROBLEM'S SOLVED.

Mermaid Aster

SOON IT'S LONG AND CURLY.

Mermaids Prentiss, Bumbrake

SOON YOU'RE ACTING GIRLY.

Mermaid Group

EACH ARROWTOOTH AND AHI,
EACH MANLY MAHI-MAHI,

All

ARE NOW THE COOLEST CREATURES IN THE SEA.
HOO-WEE!
TO THE SURF ADD THE TURF
FOR THE STARSTUFF MADE A MERMAID OUTTA ME.
MERMAIDS ARE WE!

> *Dance break.*

AND EACH OF US WERE MADE,
EACH HIM AND HER MADE,
INTO A –

Mermaid Stache

MERMAID!

All (*except MERMAID STACHE*)

BREAK THE OLDEST OF NATURE'S LAWS!
WE'LL NEVER BE FISH AGAIN BECAUSE –

All

STARSTUFF
MADE A MERMAID OUTTA ME!
MADE A MERMAID OUTTA ME!
MADE A MERMAID OUTTA ME!
IT MAKES YOU WHAT YOU WANNA BE!
SHOOP!

> *The MERMAIDS exit, alluringly.*

SCENE ONE

Mountaintop, Mollusk Island

A sense of enormous space, clear skies, bright sun, clean air. PETER is asleep on the Queen's trunk.

Peter *(dreaming)* That you, Molly? I'm coming! Wait for me! *(bolts upright, awake)* Molly, wait! *(realizes, alarmed)* No, not s'posed to sleep! S'posed to be guarding the trunk, not – What if she came and – *(stands on trunk and searches horizon)* I DID WHAT YOU SAID, MOL – dragged it right up a mountain! *(silence)* Nope, no Molly. *(blinded by the glare)* So . . . bright. Holy – Know what that is? That must be the sun! I'm feeling you, sun! *(realizing how much he can see)* And check – it – out!! Space. Light. Air. I'm finally FREE! *(Echo of FREE, FREE, FREE. This delights him.)* And I'm gonna have . . . freedoms! Whatever I want. *(A yellow bird enters suddenly and alights on his shoulder!)* Whoa. Hey bird, wassup? Me? Well, let's see . . . Saved the world. Got a name. Not too shabby. I just – I wonder if Teddy and Prentiss made it off the ship before it sank. I mean, how weird would it be if they – *(a chill up his spine, looks up)* Please let them be okay. *(scared now, a lost boy)* Bird, we should make a pact. I don't leave you, you don't leave me. Deal? *(The bird flies off.)* No! Come back! I don't wanna be alone! COME BACK! *(Echo of BACK, BACK, BACK. This leaves him desolate, but he tries to rally.)* Hey, fine. No Molly, no Teddy, no Prentiss . . . so what? This is perfect. Nobody's after me with a stick. Nothing between me and the sky. I can just be a boy for a while. It's all I want anyway. *(giving in to the lost feeling)* I gotta get outta here!

> *TED staggers on.*

Ted   Sorry, did you wanna be alone?

Peter   No! Stay with me.

Ted   Good answer.

Peter   *(to heaven)* Thank you!

> *PRENTISS appears.*

Prentiss   You ready for this? Teddy floats! We jumped overboard and I held on to Teddy, and the two of us *bobbed* all the way here!

Peter   Prentiss!

Prentiss   No-name!

Peter   I got one now. It's Peter.

Ted   Solid.

Prentiss   Whatever.

> *PETER stands atop the trunk and has a good look around.*

Peter   Look, the *Wasp*! Way out there, you see it? It's still in one piece.

Prentiss   Oh no – I see where this is going.

Ted   Where's Mother?

Prentiss   For the love of – her name is Molly! And she probably drowned.

> *TED is instantly bereft. PETER instinctively comforts him.*

Peter   No! She dove off the ship as it went down. She's like a real swimmer. I think maybe she made it to the

Wasp. Or maybe she's floating on what's left of the *Neverland* –

> *Split scene: MRS. BUMBRAKE and ALF, adrift on* Neverland *flotsam.*

Mrs. Bumbrake Ride this wreckage, Romeo! Get us to shore and make it fast!

Alf You want speed? Find me a sail!

Mrs. Bumbrake We'll end up in China drifting like this. And I'm in no mood for moo shoo, Alf! Tried it once – went through me like the winter wind in Wessex!

> *ALF and MRS. BUMBRAKE float off.*

Peter *(looking down the mountain)* Or maybe Molly's down there, in the jungle.

> *Jungle noises threaten. The BOYS consider this.*

Prentiss I say we wait for her up here.

Peter *(summoning his courage)* C'mon! Help me hide the trunk, and we'll find some branches down the beach.

Ted At some point we're gonna need food.

> *PETER and PRENTISS hide the trunk.*

Peter Branches. What we need are branches.

Ted *(spies a pineapple)* Hey, I think I found some – *(sniffs it)* Sweet! *(tries to bite into it)* Ow!

Prentiss Branches, branches . . . guy's got a jones for branches –

Peter To build a raft, you know, so we can float out to the *Wasp*. We get to the *Wasp*, Molly's father'll have to take us.

Prentiss Where?

Peter Home. *(offers his hand)* C'mon – everybody holds hands and nobody gets lost. Clear?

Ted Crystal. *(to PRENTISS)* Ew. Your hand's all sweaty.

Prentiss Yeah, 'cuz perspiration's the mark of true leadership.

> *The sunlight disappears as the BOYS head down into the dark jungle.*

SCENE TWO

Jungle

> *The BOYS cling to each other as they enter the heart of darkness.*

Peter Are we good?

Ted, Prentiss Yes!

Ted You there, Peter?

Peter Here! You there, Ted?

Ted Present!

Peter You there, Prentiss? *(Nothing.)* Prentiss? You there? *(Nothing.)* Teddy, you holding on to Prentiss? *(Nothing.)* Teddy? *(realizing his hand is empty)* Guys? Where is everybody??

> *And suddenly, they're separated, lost deep in the jungle! A tribal chant begins as strange faces appear and disappear from behind giant foliage.*

Mollusks VINO BIANCO! TREBBIANO! MOSCAT! PINOT GRIGIO!

Prentiss You said hang on to each other, Peter!

Mollusks GNOCCHI!

Ted Where are you, Peter?

Mollusks CANNOLI!

Peter I'm here, Ted!

Mollusks GNOCCHI!

Ted I'm scared, Peter!
Mollusks CANNOLI!
Prentiss I can't see a thing!
Mollusks GNOCCHI!
Ted Help! Gorillas!
Stache Oh, hello!
Peter Who was that?
Fighting Prawn CANNELLONI!
Mollusks CHIANTI!
Smee It's Smee, sir!
Fighting Prawn LINGUINI!
Mollusks VINO ROSSO! MONTEPULCIANO!
Stache Hot enough for ya?
Ted *(re: the pineapple)* How do you eat this?
Mollusks TOCAI E DOLCETTO!
Stache There! Footprints!
Prentiss Something's chasing me!
Fighting Prawn MONTEPULCIANO!
Mollusks MONTEPULCIANO!
Peter Who's that? What the – ?
Fighting Prawn CHIANTI!
Stache I'm right behind you!
Mollusks LINGUINI!
Stache And I want that trunk!
Smee D'ya want some tea?
Mollusks LINGUINI!
Stache And a biscuit, Smee!
Ted Help, I'm hungry!
Prentiss Help, I'm lost!
Stache I'm gonna find you!
Mollusks CHIANTI!
Peter I'll find you, Ted! Keep heading down!
Stache I'm sweating, Smee!

Prentiss Which way is down?
Peter Prentiss! Teddy! Guys! You hear me??
Ted HUNGRY, PETER!
Stache WANT THAT TREASURE!
Prentiss I'M THE LEADER!
Smee WANT THAT TREASURE!
Ted, Prentiss HELP ME, PETER!
Stache, Smee WANT THAT TRUNK!

> *MOLLY suddenly appears from behind a tree.*

Molly World-class swimmer that we know me to be, I reached the island in record time! I'm awfully glad I saved the boy, even if Daddy's furious. Saving the whole world's a bit abstract for a thirteen-year-old. Putting a human face on it makes it more jolly. *(adjusting herself)* Oh, this training bra is so irksome! *(fixes it)* Now, I really must fetch Daddy's trunk and bring it back to the *Wasp*, or my first-ever mission'll be my last. Don't worry, Peter, wherever you are! I'll find you!

Mollusks VINO ROSSO! MONTEPULCIANO! TOCAI E DOLCETTO!

> *FIGHTING PRAWN, King of the Mollusks, reveals himself. He wears a British top hat with a green feather in the band.*

Fighting Prawn PRIMI PRANZO – DOPO GABINETTO! *(realizing the BOYS don't understand)* Hallo. I am King of this island, and you boys are my prisoners. *("Seize them!")* LASAGNA!

> *The MOLLUSKS raise a great hue and cry as they surround the BOYS with spears.*

SCENE THREE

Mollusk Territory

Fighting Prawn   You three will do nicely.

Ted   *(surprised)* You speak English!

Fighting Prawn   If I must. *Préférez-vous que je parle français ?*

Prentiss   But you're savages!

Fighting Prawn   *(darkly)* We Mollusks are no savages. I know where savagery is, boy. When I was young man, English landed here, took me to *your* island in chains. Many long years I serve as kitchen slave in Not-So-Great Britain. Until by kindness of fate –

Hawking Clam   – a shipwreck brought my father back to Mollusk Island.

Fighting Prawn   Yes. In your language, my name is Fighting Prawn. This is my son, Hawking Clam. *(The MOLLUSKS hail their royal family with a brief chant.)*
My son shall wear this hat once worn
By my brutal British master.
For years, I was his kitchen slave.
He beat me raw, but I was brave
And one day put him in his grave
With a plate of poisoned pasta!

    The MOLLUSKS appreciate the ritual.

Fighting Prawn   Thank you.

Hawking Clam   Come, it is time.

Prentiss   Time?

Fighting Prawn Feeding time.

Ted Feeding time, finally!

Hawking Clam Not where you eat, piggy boy. Where you are *eaten*.

Fighting Prawn You must answer to the law: The Law of Mister Grin.

Prentiss Who's Mister Grin?

Hawking Clam We worship him, and he protects us from foreign troublemakers.

Fighting Prawn Come, we feed you now to vicious crocodile.

A terrible roar from off! The BOYS are terrified!

Peter WAIT!!! Please don't feed us to any crocodile. First – first take us to Mister Grin.

Fighting Prawn Crocodile is Mister Grin. *("Take them!")* PASTA!

Peter *(urgently)* Wait! We can give you great gift!

Fighting Prawn *("Release them!") ANTI*-PASTA! *(to PETER)* You said "gift"?

Peter A story – yeah, we'll give you a bedtime story. *Sleeping Beauty*. Right, guys?

Ted *Sleeping Beauty*, yeah. The thing is, I nodded off before the end.

Peter *(sotto voce to TED)* Maybe they will too, and we can get outta here! *(to FIGHTING PRAWN)* We give you story, you let us live, and we leave your island. Deal?

Fighting Prawn Okeydokey. But if I am not entertained, it's Mister Grin for all of you!! Assume the position! *(The MOLLUSKS sit.)* You have one minute!

Ted *(stricken)* One minute? What'm I supposed to do in one minute? I can't transform, I can't inhabit the character –

Act Two: Scene Three

Fighting Prawn Bring me the holy relic of my captivity!

Hawking Clam Here, Mighty Father. The kitchen timer.

> *HAWKING CLAM hands over the timer. FIGHTING PRAWN winds it.*

Fighting Prawn One minute, starting . . . NOW!

> *We hear a* Jeopardy-*like tick-tock under the boys' presentation:*

Prentiss Um . . . One at a time –

Ted *(remembering MOLLY)* Once *upon* a time – that's how they always start! Upon a time, upon a time!!

Fighting Prawn Tick-tock, tick-tock . . . hungry, Mister Grin?

> *Mister Grin roars!*

Prentiss Okay, okay! Once *upon* a time, there was a beautiful baby Princess *(cries)* Waaah!

> *One of the MOLLUSKS pokes TED, scaring him into action.*

Ted And an evil witch with a curse: A-ha-ha!

Prentiss Waaah!

Ted A-ha-ha!

> *PETER slaps PRENTISS – move it along!*

Prentiss Waaah!

Ted A-ha-ha!

> *PRENTISS smacks TED. They start to smack each other. PETER interrupts with:*

Peter And the curse was very terrible, for every time the baby cried –

Prentiss Waaah!

Peter – the whole kingdom would fall asleep!

> *PETER snores grossly then conducts the following:*

Prentiss Waaah!

Peter *(snores)*

Ted A-ha-ha!

Prentiss Waaah!

Peter *(snores)*

Ted A-ha-ha!

Prentiss Waaah!

Peter *(snores)*

Ted A-ha-ha!

Peter, Prentiss, Ted *(edging away to safety, singing)*
AND BEAUTY WAS HER NAME-OH!

> *Mister Grin roars! The BOYS, frightened, return to their "stage."*

Prentiss So the King marched over to his favorite horse!

Ted *(becoming a horse)* Naaayyy!

Prentiss *(jumping on TED's back)* And he rode to the tallest tree – *(PETER assumes the shape of a tree. TED and PRENTISS gallop to him.)* And he climbed up to speak to the wise old owl!

Ted *(becoming an owl, perched on PETER's arm-branch)* Whooo?

Prentiss The King, a real leader, sorta like me –

Ted *(as horse)* Naaayyy!

> *TED drops PRENTISS hard.*

Prentiss Focus, piggy boy!

Ted *(deeply insulted)* PIGGY BOY?!?

> *TED goes for PRENTISS but accidentally smacks PETER.*

Peter Sticky pudding!

Ted *(fainting)* Sticky pudding, it's so good . . .

> *Mister Grin roars!*

Fighting Prawn Fifteen seconds, Mister Grin!

The BOYS press on, now with courtly elegance.

Ted And soon the Princess was old enough to talk –

Prentiss "Hi. I'm sixteen, I'm beautiful, and I'm in the market for something long-term . . ."

Peter But nobody could stay awake long enough to kiss her!

Prentiss *(as a record slowing down)* And everybody got so sleeepy all of a suddennnn . . .

The BOYS give a big snore in unison.

Ted And that's the story of Sticky Pudding – *(faints again)*

Peter, Prentiss SLEEPING BEAUTY!

Molly *(not able to stand this any longer, comes out of hiding)* That's not the end! They missed the whole emotional arc of the story!

Peter *(to MOLLY)* Where'd you come from??

Fighting Prawn Goody, another English! *(DING! from the kitchen timer.)* And your minute is up!

Mister Grin roars! MOLLY and the BOYS tremble.

Peter You shoulda stayed hidden, Molly!

The MOLLUSKS gasp!

Molly You abused the concept of the theater collective – it was too much for me.

Mollusks *(rocking with laughter)* Molly! Molly! Molly!

Molly Although Ted has real talent.

Prentiss Hey, I have talent!

Ted *(Sally Field at the Oscars)* They liked me! They really liked me!

Mollusks Molly! Molly! Molly!

Peter What's so funny?

69

Fighting Prawn You called her "Molly"!

Molly Well, it's my name. Molly. *(The MOLLUSKS giggle.)* What?

Fighting Prawn In our language, "Molly" means squid poop.

> *The MOLLUSKS howl with laughter.*

Hawking Clam WAIT! *(getting back to the matter at hand)* Entertained, Mighty Father?

> *FIGHTING PRAWN hands the kitchen timer to PRENTISS.*

Fighting Prawn First prize – you got me with squid poop. Two thumbs up! Two thumbs way up!

Peter So you let us live, right? That was the deal.

Prentiss *(finishing the thought to close the deal)* Which is so great, see, 'cuz you need us! We can do all the things you guys don't wanna do anymore. We're foreigners – that's what we're for!

Fighting Prawn Nice try. But, the law is the law! All English must die! *("Kill them!")* CALAMARI!

> *The MOLLUSKS point their spears at MOLLY and the BOYS.*

SCENE FOUR

Mister Grin's Cage

Narrator Aster Such life and death decisions are generally made *by* the English, not *for* the English. Worse yet, the walls of Mister Grin's cage are very high. Too high for any boy or girl to climb. Too dark to see the crocodile in front of your face. And those hard things the boys are sitting on – they feel like bones. All in all, it's a bad day to be British.

MOLLY and the BOYS cower and huddle. TED clings to his pineapple. From an adjacent enclosure, Mister Grin roars!

Prentiss Teddy, I hope that was your stomach.

Ted I wanna go home.

Prentiss What home?

Peter He made a deal with us, and he lied, just like they always do. I hate grown-ups!

Ted Do something, Prentiss! You're the leader! Have a plan!

Prentiss *(grabs the timer and shouts to Mister Grin)* Eat the kitchen timer and leave us alone!!

PRENTISS throws the kitchen timer deep into the cage. Mister Grin roars! A chomping sound, then "tick-tock, tick-tock . . ." PRENTISS collapses in tears.

Ted Great, now we can count the seconds 'til we die.

Peter *(building to a tantrum)* This is all your fault, Molly. Makin' me feel like this big man who's gonna save the world! Well, I'm not a big man, and I can't save anything!

Molly Not a good time for a hissy, Peter. You failed, so you try again. My father always says that.

Peter THEN LET *HIM* SAVE US!

Mister Grin roars! The BOYS cringe.

Molly Should've given the trunk to my father. Then he'd have all the starstuff and – *(remembers her amulet)* Molly, you idiot!

Prentiss She's cracking up.

Ted No, maybe she has a plan.

Molly I do! I have a plan!

71

Mister Grin roars! Giant red eyes appear!

Prentiss *(shrieking)* Eyes! Look at the eyes!

Molly *(undeterred)* This amulet is my plan! The starstuff inside is my plan! *(pointedly, to PETER)* You with us, boy, or is it sulk-and-die?

Peter I'm with you, I'm with you.

Molly Good. *(kisses PETER)* It's a better team with you on it, Peter.

> *PETER is stunned. But Mister Grin's enclosure ratchets open!*

Prentiss HERE IT COMES!

Molly Now, Peter! Get him to open wide!!

> *Roar!!! TED and PRENTISS scream! PETER flings himself into action before he can think better of it.*

Peter *(waving his arms)* Tasty boy! Fresh today! Come and eat me!!

> *Mister Grin opens his gaping maw.*

Molly Duck!!

> *MOLLY throws her amulet in Mister Grin's mouth. A moment of extreme tension. And then . . . a satisfied burp.*

Narrator Prentiss The ringing of bells fills the air.

Narrator Ted And Mister Grin begins to coo, gurgle –

Narrator Peter – and GROW!

Narrator Molly Bigger every second!

Narrator Peter Giant mouth!

Narrator Prentiss Giant teeth!

Narrator Ted Giant appetite!

Narrator Molly Until the crocodile shatters through his bamboo enclosure –

Narrators Peter, Ted, Prentiss, Molly – an airborne

leviathan!

> *The vast fangs of the airborne MISTER GRIN appear, chomping.*

Peter   So basically I'm thinking: Let's —

Ted   — get outta —

Prentiss   — HERE!!!

> *The BOYS and MOLLY run off, pursued by the giant Mister Grin. FIGHTING PRAWN appears with HAWKING CLAM in another part of the jungle.*

Fighting Prawn   Those dirty, filthy, rotten, stinking English!

Hawking Clam   They ruin bedtime story!

Fighting Prawn   English ruin everything! Why they make Mister Grin so big?

Hawking Clam   We catch and kill them, Mighty Father!

Fighting Prawn   But leave Peter Boy and Little Miss Squid Poop for me. Them, Fighting Prawn will butterfly and deep fat fry! *("After them!")* SCAMPI!!

Mollusks   *(chanting from off)* BUTTERFLY AND DEEP FAT FRY! BUTTERFLY AND DEEP FAT FRY!! BUTTERFLY AND DEEP FAT FRY!!!

> *HAWKING CLAM, FIGHTING PRAWN, and the rest of the MOLLUSKS pursue the boys, running deeper into the jungle.*

SCENE FIVE

Beach

STACHE enters, carried on by SMEE.

Stache Set me down, you dozy prat. I can't go another step.

Smee That trunk is hard to find, Cap'n.

Stache So it is. Elusive as the melody in a Philip Glass opera.

Smee Rest yerself a while. Smee'll track yer treasure solo.

Stache Negaroni. We'll trick the pewling spawn and make 'em bring it hither. But how to do it? How to smoke 'em out –

Smee We could lure 'em, Cap'n!

Stache Lure 'em, y'say?

Smee *(smacks himself on the head)* Stupid idea, Smee. Stupid, stupid!

Stache Lure 'em, yes. Down here to the butch.

Smee Beach.

Stache Beach. In which case, we shall need –

Smee A magnet. A really big one. That'll attract 'em!

Stache Smee, Smee . . . I know your heart's in the right place, but – *(A distant ROAR.)* Smee, you've been hitting the three-bean couscous again.

Smee 'Tweren't I, Cap'n.

Stache Wait! I have it!

Smee *(sees something shocking overhead)* Oh, Captain?

Stache Lucky for me you saved your ukulele!

Smee   Captain Stache!!!!!

Stache   A siren's song is what we need, Smee, and you're going to be the luscious siren – *(sees Mister Grin)* WHOA! BIG CROC! *(runs off)*

Smee   He's chewing all the scenery, sir.

Stache   *(runs on)* Not in my scene, he ain't! *(to Mister Grin)* Spare me the theatrics, y'reptilian ham! *(Mister Grin roars monstrously!)* Abandon spleen!

Smee   Scene!

Stache   Scene!

Smee, Stache   Abandon scene!

STACHE and SMEE run off.

SCENE SIX

Jungle's Edge

MOLLY runs on, followed by the BOYS, who are winded, exhausted, and collapsing. MOLLY continues running, and is gone.

Peter   Grab anything that looks like it'll float! We're gettin' outta here.

Molly   *(runs back on, checking her pulse and other vitals)* No – first, take me to the trunk. Remember the mission.

Peter   Forget the trunk – the trunk is safe. What we need is a raft!

Molly   It's not your decision, Peter. Protect the trunk – that's the mission!

Peter   You have to have it your way, don't you! *(A bright, strong light blinks in their eyes.)* What is that – ?

Prentiss Blinking fierce – !

> *From out on the* Wasp, *ASTER signals MOLLY.*

Molly It's Father! Father – oh, good! He's signaling me all the way from the *Wasp*!!

Ted What's it mean?

Molly He's using Norse Code! It's Norse Code, everyone!

> *PRENTISS starts laughing.*

Prentiss Um – sorry – I think you mean Morse Code.

Molly *(not amused)* Not Morse Code. Norse Code! From Norway. The ancient Viking signaling system.

Prentiss That's ridiculous.

Peter What's he saying?

Molly Unless I miss my guess, he's saying, "*Marla bella furna seena heina furna.*" And then he says, "*Un, gettsie Molly doozee blingen.*" That's: "First, take Molly to the trunk." "*Coom heller high water.*" That's: "Remember the mission."

Peter Very convenient.

Molly "*Un gettsie blingen doozee plakken.*" That's: "Take the trunk down to the beach." "*Marla bella furna*" – "Father'll be there with the longboat." "*Seena heina furna*" – "We'll be" "*heina furna*" – um, "safe, if we can just get past the pirates and make it to the beach." "*Den tooren inder flanken essen, neckon freska tudor! Nayben nay benessa, nay benanka, binta rubalenka sinkin-hookin keep de motor cookin, anka Danke, Papa.*" – "Love, Daddy."

> *MOLLY takes a proud, deep breath of linguistic expertise.*

Prentiss Women are tricky, man.

Peter I feel kinda stupid not knowing Norwegian.

Molly It isn't a contest. Though, if it were, I'd win.

Peter   And the running – you're really fast. Better than me.

Molly   Well, you're a better leader.

Peter   Really?

Molly   No. *(laughs, then)* C'mon, take me to the trunk!

Mollusks   *(from off)* BUTTERFLY AND DEEP FAT FRY! BUTTERFLY AND DEEP FAT FRY!!

Molly   The Mollusks!

Ted, Prentiss   The Mollusks!!

Mollusks   *(from off)* THE MOLLUSKS!!!

Molly   We'll have to outrun them!

Peter   Take the guys with you! I'll get the Mollusks to follow me!

Ted   Hear that, Prentiss? That's the sound of a leader!

TED and PRENTISS run for their lives.

Molly   I'm not leaving you!

Peter   Afraid I'll beat you to the top?

Molly   As if! *(runs off, then returns)* Bravo, Peter.

MOLLY runs off again. PETER is exultant at having pleased her. He waves his arms to attract attention.

Peter   Here I am, Mollusks! Come and get me!

SCENE SEVEN

Up the Mountain

PETER begins running. The MOLLUSKS chase him, thirsty for blood!

Narrator   Fighting   Prawn   Bounding through the jungle and up the mountain, Peter's thoughts are only of outrunning the natives.

Peter   Try'n catch me, Fighting Prawn!

Narrator Stache   And the faster he runs, the further he gets –

Narrator Aster   – from the terrible beatings –

Narrator Prentiss   – the boarded-up garrets –

Narrator Peter   – the smell and the filth and the dark of the cave!

Narrator Smee   And the further he runs, the more that he smiles –

Narrator Fighting Prawn   – from saving the others –

Narrator Stache   – and being a leader –

Narrator Molly   – 'til, panting and jumping and practically flying, Peter feels something entirely new!

> *Freeze the chase!*

Peter   Alive!

> *Unfreeze the chase!*

Narrator Aster   And all of a sudden, surrounding his head –

> *The yellow bird appears among a flock of yellow birds and flits around PETER's head as he runs.*

Peter   *(swatting)* Get outta my face, bird. I can't see where I'm going!

Narrator Molly   And that's when he misses a ledge and falls!

Peter   MOLLY . . . !

Narrator Scott   And down and down he bumps and bruises –

Narrator Fighting Prawn   – leaving the natives with no one to chase.

Narrator Hawking Clam   Banging and buffeting –

Narrator Prentiss   – down a deep crevice, as gravity beckons –

Narrator Scott – crooking her finger and winking her eye, and Peter falling for her big time.

Narrator Alf And rushing up to meet him –

Narrator Peter – is a solid sheet of glass!

Narrators SPLASH!

> *PETER splash-lands in a pool of golden water.*

Narrator Scott His brutal fall is broken –

Narrator Aster – and not his neck –

Narrator Ted – and not by glass at all –

Narrator Fighting Prawn – but by a shimmering lake of golden water, far, far underground.

Narrator Aster He should've been drowning, should've been afraid, but he was neither drowning nor afraid. Peter bobbed to the surface, safe as you please, and began to get his bearings.

Narrator Stache And the water was thick like oil, and full of light, too – and warm, like a rich man's bath.

Narrator Prentiss And looking down fondly at Peter was –

Peter – a mermaid!

SCENE EIGHT

Grotto

Perched on a rocky ledge above the water, a grand dame of a MERMAID looks down at PETER.

Teacher Well, well . . . nice of you to drop in. I'm Teacher – that's what I'm called. And yes, I speak

English. I know your name is Peter. I know a lot of things.

Peter Where am I?

Teacher In a hurry.

Peter That's right . . . I was running away from —

Teacher The Mollusk natives.

Peter They're trying to kill us! And we just wanna get home!

Teacher Yeah, life is complicated.

Peter I was gonna build a raft to get to the *Wasp*, but Molly's father is —

Teacher You don't need a raft to get home, and you don't need the *Wasp*. All you need is starstuff.

Peter How'd you know about — ?

Teacher Listen to Teacher. When you rode the trunk to this island, seawater seeped inside. Then the starstuff in the trunk enchanted the water. Then the water enchanted the fish in the wake of the trunk. Then the waves —

Peter But how'd you know about — ?

Teacher I'm not finished. Then the waves washed the water right into this grotto, where I was swimmin'.

Peter So you used to be a fish?

Teacher Scotch salmon. This is way cooler, FYI. *(pointedly)* The starstuff'll change you, too. It makes you what you want to be.

Peter But I just wanna be a boy for a while. Couldn't I just be a boy?

Teacher Well, I suppose . . . once you sit in the starstuff —

Peter Yeah, then what?

Teacher Sky's the limit. You could even fly yourself home maybe, just like you dreamed.

Peter   And find a family.

Teacher   In which case, you're going to need something. A name.

Peter   Instead of Peter?

Teacher   In addition to. A family name. *(calling to the grotto)* And we've come up with a good one, haven't we?

Narrator Alf   And in the grotto, or in the water, or both — an echo, or a voice or both, seemed to answer:

Narrators   *(as echo, gently)* PAN.

Teacher   What are you, boy?

Peter   I'm Peter.

Narrators   *(as echo, louder)* PAN.

Peter   *(disappointed)* Pan? You mean like in the kitchen?

Teacher   You are just too cute. I mean two things, actually. First is fun and frolic — anarchy, mischief, all the things a boy likes to —

Peter   *(he's down with that)* Fun! Okay! I'm Peter Pan.

Teacher   There. You're changing already.

Peter   You said Pan means two things. What's the second thing?

Teacher   Shouldn't you be on your way? Molly's going to beat you to that trunk.

Narrators   MOLLY!

Peter   *(quickly out from the golden pool of water)* THE TRUNK!

> *PETER dashes off. Thunder! Lightning! Meanwhile . . .*

81

SCENE NINE

Mountaintop

MOLLY, PRENTISS, and TED have retrieved the trunk.

Molly WINNERS – YES! We beat him to the top! We came in first – I'll make that very clear when he gets here.

Prentiss If he gets here.

Molly Of course he'll get here! He has to!

Prentiss Face facts, Molly. The natives got him, and I feel terrible. *(TED slams the pineapple on his leg. PRENTISS sees him wince.)* We *all* feel terrible, but Peter's out of the running. Which means we can finally settle the question of what, for a better word, one might deem "leadership."

Ted *(pointing at something far away)* Cripes! A floating tomato!

Prentiss Say what?

Molly That red dot on the horizon!

Split scene: ALF and MRS. BUMBRAKE enter on the raft, her red flannel bloomers catching the wind and carrying them boldly toward Mollusk Island.

Alf Betty, you're a genius! Whee-ho! A vast behind!

Mrs. Bumbrake My bloomers have stood up to stronger wind than this! Full speed ahead!

As quickly as they appeared, the raft, ALF, MRS. BUMBRAKE, and her dignity are gone.

Molly They're safe. That's good. *(remembering)* I wish Peter were here. *(THUNDER! LIGHTNING!)* The mission comes first. Get the trunk to the beach. Now, move it!

The COMPANY enters as the rainstorm begins.

Narrator Grempkin The night that Ted and Prentiss spend dragging the trunk down the mountain is worse than any at the orphanage –

Narrator Ted – because the rain isn't like the rain in England.

Narrator Prentiss It falls like stones and hurts your head!

Narrator Stache And you can't see, because there's trees –

Narrator Aster – in front of trees –

Narrator Bumbrake – surrounded by trees smacking your face.

Narrator Molly And you can't breathe –

Narrator Alf – from the bugs –

Narrator Peter – and the beetles –

Narrator Grempkin – flying –

Narrator Ted – crawling –

Narrator Scott – sticky –

Narrator Bumbrake – crunchy –

Narrator Aster – and they're in your mouth –

Narrator Stache – and up your nose –

Narrator Molly – and down your front!

Narrator Prentiss So you take cover and wait out the storm –

Narrator Stache – but you can forget about sleep –

Narrator Bumbrake – 'cuz it's way too scary out here and there's a trunk to save –

Narrator Aster   – and you still have to reach the beach!

> *MOLLY is revealed guarding the trunk. PRENTISS and TED are sound asleep on the jungle floor.*

Molly   I said forget about sleep! Teddy!

> *Suddenly . . . PETER!*

Peter   He's spark out.

Molly   *(startled)* Peter! Oh, Peter! I thought –

> *MOLLY throws her arms around PETER's neck. They're ecstatic, reunited, like kids.*

Peter   The most incredible thing – you won't believe – I met this –

> *PETER and MOLLY stop, embarrassed.*

Molly   Right. Well. Good to see you, Peter. Shall we wake the boys?

Peter   Been kind of a long day. Leave 'em be.

Molly   Just us then.

Peter   Yeah. Just us. *(jiggles the trunk's lock)* We should open the trunk – make sure the starstuff's okay.

Molly   Oh no, that's not, no –

Peter   I wanna sit in the starstuff –

Molly   Very dangerous – exposure to so much of it.

Peter   I don't care!

Molly   Well, I do! I was so worried. We waited and waited. I told them you'd come. We waited – *(darker, sitting on the ground)* and then the rain and the dark and I was so worried –

Peter   *(leaning in)* I'm here. *(sits next to MOLLY)* Do you think I've changed?

Molly   You're dirtier.

Peter   So, I've been meaning to ask you about the, um . . .

about that, uh – you know – about that thing you
did –

Molly What thing?

Peter The kiss, okay? The kiss.

Molly What kiss?

Peter The kiss! The one you gave me!

Molly Oh, the kiss.

Peter "What kiss," she says.

Molly Well, what about it?

Peter Nobody's ever wanted to kiss me, that's all –

Molly Want to? I didn't want to, we were about to be
eaten alive and –

Peter I mean, I was just sitting there and you grabbed
me –

Molly Oh for heaven's sake, such a fuss! Didn't you
like it?

Peter No, it was –

Molly *(standing, upset)* You didn't like it. You didn't like
it, and now you're telling me you didn't like it!
Unbelievable.

Peter I'm not saying I didn't like it –

Ted *(dreaming)* Mmm . . . pork.

Molly *(keeping her voice down so as not to wake TED)* Then
what're you saying?

Peter I'm guess I'm saying – I guess I'm asking –

Molly You stop that right now. I won't answer any such
question. You're inclining toward the sentimental and
that's all well and good for a boy, but the fact is –

Peter Inclining toward what?

Molly – we girls can't afford to be sentimental. We must
instead be strong. *(lifts herself to sit atop the trunk)* And
when I marry, my husband will have to –

Peter MARRY? Whoa, you thought I was asking you to –

Molly Not you, you swot. Uch, the ego. *(starting again)* And when I marry, I shall make it very clear to this person – that sentimentality is not on the calendar. He will have to lump it or leave it. And if he should leave, I'll stay a spinster and pin my hair back and volunteer weekends at hospital. And I will love words for their own sake, like "hyacinth" and "Piccadilly" and "onyx." And I'll have a good old dog, and think what I like, and be part of a different sort of family, with friends, you know? – who understand that things are only worth what you're willing to give up for them. *(then)* Even if I – in the face of death, I may have – you know –

Peter *(sits next to MOLLY)* Wanted to?

Molly I didn't say that.

Peter *(gently, sweetly, holds MOLLY's hand)* Got it.

Molly Good.

Peter *(absorbing)* Wow.

> *A moment. They suddenly seem older. MOLLY stifles a yawn.*

Molly *(giving in to exhaustion)* You know, I might just – now you're here – rest my eyes for a little –

> *MOLLY hops off the trunk and curls up in front of the lock. Instantly, she's asleep. Gingerly, PETER tries to jiggle the lock open. The noise disturbs PRENTISS.*

Prentiss *(dreaming)* No, Molly, no! The leader has to be a – !

> *PRENTISS awakens. PETER's moment has passed, and he runs off.*

Molly *(rubs her eyes)* Where's Peter?

Prentiss The Mollusks got him, remember?

It is now morning. TED sits up, shielding his eyes from the dawn's glare.

Ted   Is that the sun? What's for breakfast? *(licks the pineapple)* Ow!

Narrator Alf   Did he say the sun? But if you can see the sun coming up –

Narrator Bumbrake   If you can see the sky at all –

Molly   We must be very near the beach! C'mon, boys! We made it!

The strumming of a ukulele is heard, as MOLLY, PRENTISS, and TED push the trunk to the beach.

SCENE TEN

Beach

The sun is coming up over the horizon, revealing jagged debris from the wreck of the Neverland, *including a piece of the ship's bow. A lone mermaid, who has seen better days (SMEE in disguise), plays a siren song on her ukulele.*

Mermaid/Smee   *(singing)*
COME TO ME, YE SHIPWRECKED SAILORS.
LOOKEE HERE, YE WAVE-TOSSED WHALERS.
OOH AH! OOH AH!
SAILOR BOY, KEEP SAILING NEAR ME.
CLOSER NOW, SO'S YOU CAN HEAR ME.
AS YER SHIP BREAKS TO BITS,
FROM YER DECK, FOR A SEC,
YOU CAN SEE MY LOVELY –

STACHE bursts on!

Stache   No, no, no, no, no. The object is to lure 'em, Smee – not send 'em into psychoanalysis! *(pulls SMEE's wig off)* No, simple's best. We go to Plan B: The Poisoned Fruitcake. The hateful brats arrive – empty beach, tempting morsel. Maybe a note: "Feel free, tuck in." They eat it, they die –

Smee   They come, Cap'n!

Stache   Let's kill us some kiddies, Smee!

Smee   So nasty! So very nasty!

> *STACHE and SMEE disappear, just as TED and PRENTISS enter, exhausted.*

Ted   So hungry. So very hungry.

> *MOLLY enters, pulling the trunk.*

Prentiss   *(pointing off to the lagoon)* There's the longboat.

Molly   But where's Daddy?

> *Enter STACHE in disguise, hawking a poisoned fruitcake.*

Stache   Get yer tasty fruitcake here! Get yer nice slice o'fruitcake!

Ted   Omigosh, YYYEEESSSSSS!!!!!

> *TED dives for the cake, but MOLLY stops him.*

Molly   NO, TED! DON'T!

Stache   Fresh out of the bakehouse! Yummy Yum Yum –

> *MOLLY rips off STACHE's disguise.*

Molly   You're The Black Stache. My father will have your guts for garters.

Stache   *(mock fear)* Ooooooh! *(calling off)* Plan C, Smee!

> *SMEE runs on with another poisoned fruitcake.*

Smee   Poisoned fruitcake, brats?

Stache   That was Plan B, Smee. *(bustling him off)* Get rid of it.

> *SMEE exits with two fruitcakes.*

Ted   WAIT! Just a sliver!

Stache   Too latey, matey! PLAN C!

> *SMEE and the PIRATES bring on two prisoners: MRS. BUMBRAKE and ALF.*

Mrs. Bumbrake   Molly!

Molly   Oh, Mrs. Bumbrake! Mrs. Bumbrake –

Mrs. Bumbrake   Bum-broken's more like it! They grabbed us by the mangroves when we landed, the ruffians. Alf was valiant, heroic –

Stache   Ruffians?? How dare you, madam. We are no ruffians.

Smee   Why, we've never even been to Ruffia!

Mrs. Bumbrake   I don't care what you are, sir, I assure you.

Stache   What I am, madam? I'll tell – !

Smee   *(jumping the gun)* BLACK STACHE!

> *SMEE screams a terrible scream and runs around, until he realizes he's doing so alone.*

Stache   *(a glare at SMEE)* Thank you, Smee! *(to MOLLY)* And it is my serious intent to kill this woman until she is dead, and Alfred too, unless you leave that trunk with me and my nasty crew.

Molly   Stay right where you are, and I'll see it goes easy for you with my father.

Stache   Your daddy's not around, dearie. And there's more of us than there are of you.

Fighting Prawn *(from off)* And there's more of us than anybody! *("Surrender!")* PROSCIUTTO!

> *FIGHTING PRAWN enters with the MOLLUSKS and their prisoners: ASTER and SCOTT, bound and gagged.*

Molly Daddy! Captain Scott! Not you, too!

Fighting Prawn *(to MOLLY)* NO ENGLISH MOVE!

> *Amid the distraction, STACHE hides behind the other prisoners. MRS. BUMBRAKE gets a good look at FIGHTING PRAWN.*

Mrs. Bumbrake Prawnie – ? Prawnie, is that you?

Fighting Prawn Betty?

Mrs. Bumbrake *(as the servant she once was)* "The mistress wants more of your manicotti."

Fighting Prawn *(as the servant he once was)* "And a pasta fazool – "

Mrs. Bumbrake " – to make you drool!"

Fighting Prawn Betty Bumbrake, it's you! *(to assembled PRISONERS)* This woman only English kind to me when I was kitchen slave!

> *HAWKING CLAM pushes ASTER forward.*

Mrs. Bumbrake Be a prince, Prawnie, and let Lord Aster loose.

Fighting Prawn You are English, so I'll choose my words carefully. No.

Mrs. Bumbrake But Prawnie –

Fighting Prawn You English invade our island, now Nature's Laws are all *focaccia!*

Molly Because of the contents of this trunk, Your Highness. Release my father, and we'll take the trunk off the island. Nature restored. Mollusks live happily ever after!

STACHE grabs FIGHTING PRAWN from behind, holding his straight razor at the king's throat.

Stache "Happily ever after" my kebab knife! *(to MOLLY)* You, kitty cat! Bring the trunk here or I cut the savage's throat.

Molly *(trapped in a moral dilemma)* That's a terrible choice – I have a sacred duty!

Stache Take yer time. I'll count to three – THREE!

Echo (Peter) THREE . . . Three . . . three . . .

Stache What's that? An ECHO?

Echo (Peter) ECHO . . . Echo . . . echo . . .

Stache Excellent effect! The Stache is CUNNING!

Echo (Peter) CUNNING . . . Cunning . . .

Stache The Stache is BEGUILING!

Echo (Peter) GUILING . . . Guiling . . .

Stache The Stache is SUPREME!

Peter I DON'T THINK SO!

STACHE is flummoxed. PETER leaps into view, holding a branch as a weapon.

Stache You.

Peter Me.

Stache Peter.

Peter Pan!

Prentiss He's alive!

Ted We're saved!

Molly *(shouting instructions)* Thrust and parry, Peter! *Attaque coulé ! Balestra !*

STACHE hands off FIGHTING PRAWN to SMEE. PETER thrusts. STACHE easily parries and sends PETER sprawling.

Stache And so we arrive in the belly of the beast.

> *STACHE holds his razor at PETER's throat, about to strike.*

Peter Teddy, throw it!

Ted Yo! Think fast! *(throws his pineapple at STACHE, who defends himself by slashing the fruit in two pieces!)* Really, after all that? *(STACHE instantly gets TED in a headlock.)* Prentiss, PRENTISS!!!

Prentiss *(rushes STACHE)* WHAT AM I DOING?? Omigod please don't hurt me, I'm just a little kid! I'm not responsible!! *(bursts into tears)*

Stache *(to TED)* Is he crying? Seriously? *(PRENTISS grabs STACHE's arm and bites his hand.)* Aaaargh! Me hand! *(STACHE drops the razor and gets PRENTISS in a headlock. MOLLY picks up Stache's razor.)* Next?

Molly *(assuming the "praying mantis" martial arts position)* Aaaaiiiiiieeeeee-hunh!

Stache *(pointing somewhere)* Oh, looky-loo! A baby koala!

Molly *(falling for it)* A koala? Oh they're just so adora – *(STACHE swipes his razor from MOLLY and gets her in a headlock.)* Unfair!

Stache *(in MOLLY's ear)* Say yer good-byes, m'dear –

Peter WAIT! Don't you want the trunk?

Molly Peter, don't!

Peter *(to PRENTISS and TED)* Are you with me, guys?

Ted Gotta save Mother.

Prentiss She's more important than some trunk.

Peter Even if I never get home.

> *The BOYS hug in sympathy and understanding, friends.*

Stache Are we quite done with the hugging and learning?

Peter Decision. *(pushes trunk to STACHE)* It's a better world with you in it, Molly. *(to STACHE)* Now, let her go.

Stache *(moved, deeply)* 'Dja note that, Smee? 'Dja see it? Genuine heroic sacrifice.

Smee *(sarcastic)* Inspiring, Cap'n. I've got gooseflesh all over.

Stache Poor Smee. How flat and unprofitable the world must seem from the deck of the *HMS Cynic. (inspired, handing MOLLY to PETER)* Go, lad. Take yer precious lady and live another day.

Molly *(bereft)* My first mission, and I've wrecked it!

Stache *(tossing key to SMEE)* Now, open it, Smee. Open, and elaborate.

Smee *(opens the trunk elaborately, then stops cold)* It's — it's —

Stache "It's"? I don't like "It's." Bollocks to "It's." *(pushes SMEE away and looks inside the trunk, a beat)* Do we detect a pattern here? Help me, the linguists among you, what's the turn of phrase?

Smee Empty, Cap'n. The trunk's empty.

Stache So it is. *(through gritted teeth)* Clean as the sheets in a convent.

Peter *(runs to see)* Empty, it can't be empty!

Molly You mean all this time —

Stache, Peter WHERE'S MY TREASURE!!

Molly The seawater got in. It must have dissolved —

Stache Moose nuggets! Gold and diamonds don't DISSOLVE!

Molly But starstuff does. Is that right, Daddy?

Aster *(incoherent due to the gag in his mouth)* Well actually, the molecular framework of starstuff begins to break down when it –

Stache *(not quite hearing)* Starbucks? Starbucks? What's Starbucks??

Molly Doesn't matter now. Nobody gets his hands on it –

Peter Nobody gets what he wants.

Stache *(pushes PETER away from the trunk)* Enough of this non-versation! *(to ASTER)* See, this is why I hate, I hate, I HATE – ! *(slams the trunk in a fury, forgetting his right hand resting on the edge; agony! as he processes the pain of having cut off his own hand)* Omigod. Omigod. Omigod. *(a few more, perhaps, and then)* Omigod. Um – wait –

Smee *(runs to STACHE)* Sir?

Stache *(through the excruciating pain)* And you are – ?

Smee Smee, sir – your right-hand man.

Stache Not anymore, Smee. Not anymore – thanks in no small part – TO THIS!! *(holds up his stump to a collective gasp!)*

Smee *(weeping)* Oh Captain, my Captain!

Stache Crocodile tears, Smee. Opine if ye would, what'm I to do now?

Smee I'm stumped, sir.

Stache You're stumped? It's all about you, isn't it? Selfy-self-self.

Smee I sir? Not me, sir –

Stache Then kindly retrieve it! *(lifts trunk lid)* I'm not leaving me hand behind for these children to paw!

Smee *(holding up a severed hand)* Retrieved, Cap'n.

Stache *(to PETER)* You! You sacrificed, willingly, for the sake of a gill.

Smee Girl.

Stache Girrrrrrl. And that was majestic! You've piqued the poet in me, Pan. What say we merge a forger?

Smee Forge a merger.

Stache THANK YOU, SMEE! *(to PETER)* Picture it, Pete. The ultimate pirate and his worthy opponent.

Peter Molly fights better than me.

Molly I run faster too.

Stache And I bet your milkshake brings all the boys to the yard! But I'm not interested. *(to PETER)* Consider the possibilities. Foes forever. Adversaries *ad neverendum.* I'm talking books, movies, Broadway –

Peter But you just tried to kill me –

Stache Don't you get it, Peter? You're my hero!

Peter Me?

Stache You're the ying to me yang. The semi to me colon. Dammit, Boy, you're the wind beneath my clippéd wing!

Peter Gee, I hadn't really –

Stache Thanks to you, I am reborn! The complete villain! O, what sublime enemies we'll be! Forget gold! Time. Time'll be our treasure. We'll fight for all eternity. We's a couple now, boo.

Peter *(negotiating)* Only if my friends go free.

Stache Oh, bravo, *bravissimo*! Give the Pan a round of – *(tries to clap his hands, but he's short one)* Smee, a little help? *(tries to clap the severed hand held by SMEE, but utterly fails, grabs it, and points it at PETER)* This is all your doing, ye loathsome Pan. You single-handedly rendered me single-handed!

Peter You cut your hand off, not me!

Stache O, pity the child who lives in a fact-based world!

(standing theatrically atop the trunk) You may think my ship has sailed, but I have an armada of options at my former fingertips. Perhaps I'll never be a concert violinist or a reliable juggler, but I can still win Wimbledon – and I can still destroy you! YOU'VE MADE YOUR BED, PAN!

Peter Go on! *(calling off)* Get the hook!!

> *ROAR! Tick-tock, tick-tock . . . Everyone looks up and cowers.*

Smee North-northwest! Enormous ticking crocodile, Cap'n! Back for another snack!

Stache Upstaging me still, ye snaggletooth'd show-off??

Smee Just not your day, sir.

Stache Hang on! I could use a killer croc on me crew. Bring the beast along, Smee.

Smee How'm I to lure 'im, sir?

Stache Give 'im the hand, y'fool! *(tosses his hand to SMEE)* Wait – best make it last. Just give 'im the finger. *(SMEE tries to pry a finger from Stache's hand as he exits.)* Adieu, Pan. But believe this: Where'er you call home, keep your back to the wall. For just when you least expect it, there I'll be! The Stache, right under yer nose! *(exits, stops, and returns for:)* Clap if you believe!

> *STACHE exits. Applause, no doubt.*

Molly *(rushes to ASTER, removes his gag, and hugs him)* Daddy! Thank goodness you're safe –

Aster Molly! My Molly.

Mollusks *(they just love saying it)* Molly! Molly! Molly!

Fighting Prawn Boy! You good son. Fighting Prawn honor that. *(puts his top hat on PETER's head)* Boy will wear hat of hero. And Fighting Prawn will bend

Mollusk law – allow all English to leave island! *(to ALF)* You be good to Betty, or I serve you up *al dente*!

Alf   Oh, we've made plans, Your Prawnness. I got down on bended knee and Missus B said –

Mrs. Bumbrake   You betcha! Betty's bound for bridal bliss!

Alf   Aye, the *HMS Bumbrake* may have a few barnacles on her bottom, but Alf'll scrape 'em off!

Mrs. Bumbrake   Don't speak, dearie. *(arms out to FIGHTING PRAWN)* Oh, Prawnie! TTFN.

Fighting Prawn   Ta-ta for now. Or in my language: TIRAMISU!

All   TIRAMISU! TIRAMISU!

> *The MOLLUSKS vanish back into the jungle.*

Scott   Len, old sport, it's back to England. And then I can finally set my sights on the South Pole.

Aster   The Antarctic?

Scott   Or my name's not Robert Falcon Scott. *(to his CREW)* Trunk to the longboat!

> *The SEAMEN carry off the empty trunk. MRS. BUMBRAKE and ALF follow them off.*

Molly   *(saluting SCOTT)* Good luck, Captain. Don't let the Norwegians beat you to it!

Scott   Nobody beats the British, little girl. Rule Britannia!

> *SCOTT exits.*

Aster   *(to MOLLY, of whom he is very proud indeed)* Not a little girl. A full-fledged Starcatcher.

Molly   *(ecstatic)* Full-fledged Starcatcher! Just like my wonderful father!

Peter   She deserves it, sir. Molly's the real hero.

Molly   Thanks, Peter.

Aster   Mission fulfilled. We're heading home!

Molly And you'll come with us! Can't they, Daddy? Can't the boys come home with us?

Prentiss Mother!

Ted I told you!

Peter And Teacher said all I needed to get home was starstuff! Ha! WRONG!

Aster Who?

Molly Who's Teacher?

Peter This tricked-out mermaid. Well, she was a fish, but she swam in the grotto and NOW WE'RE GOING HOME!

Aster Wait! What grotto?

Peter The grotto with the golden water.

Aster Did you go in that water?

Peter Yeah, it was great – all warm and tingly.

Molly *(to ASTER, realizing)* The starstuff.

Aster And he soaked in it. *(taking MOLLY aside)* We can't do this.

Molly *(fighting it)* But it already dissolved in the waves!

Aster The waves that turn fish into mermaids. I'm sorry, Peter – we can't take you with us.

Peter Why? What'd I do?

Molly But he isn't evil or greedy. And he isn't –

Aster We don't know what he is. Or what he wants to be.

Peter I just wanna be a boy for a while. That's all I ever wanted –

Molly *(defiant, to ASTER)* There, you see?

Aster With starstuff, "a while" could be a very long time.

Peter But I'll be good. I promise!

Molly The boy deserves a home!

Aster Of course he does, but – wait – Leonard, old man, you're getting slow! Peter, what if your mermaid was right?

Peter She wasn't right, and neither are you! Grown-ups lie. They lie and then they leave.

Aster I thought she said the starstuff was all you needed to get home.

Peter But I'm still here.

Aster Precisely. Did she say anything else?

Peter She said I needed a family name – so she gave me one.

Molly Pan. Pan, as in "all." *(off ASTER's look – "Wow, you actually studied your Greek!")* Probably.

Peter All?

Molly Your family name, understand? The whole island. All the ants on the beach, all the birds in the air, the mermaids, the Mollusks, the pirates, and the boys too, of course, especially the boys – they're all your family.

PETER brightens at that word.

Aster And how does that make you feel?

Peter Like – like I'm finally out of the dark.

Aster There's a name for that feeling, Peter.

Peter Home.

Aster And here you are. *(to MOLLY)* And here he'll stay.

Prentiss Yeah, me too, totally, count me in.

Ted You didn't wanna be alone, didja?

Molly *(angry)* Well, this is just so unacceptable. We Asters do not leave boys behind.

Suddenly – the yellow bird appears, and dive-bombs PETER.

Peter Whoa! That crazy bird is after me again. Whadda you want? Lemme alone!

PETER swats the bird down, covers it with his hat, and makes to stomp on it.

Aster STOP! Don't hurt that bird! *(PETER obeys and*

lowers his foot to the ground.) You're going to need something to protect you. Now, it seems to me — *(flipping over the hat and removing his amulet)* — if we take the last of the starstuff, like so — *(drops amulet in the hat, covers it, whooshes it around)* — and stir vigorously, I think it's *anti*-clockwise . . . Peter, lend a hand, whip the meringue!

Peter   *(helps stir the hat as the sound of bells fills the air)* Hey, the hat's getting all warm and tingly. Just like —

Aster   And so!

> *ASTER uncovers the hat and a Light flies out, caresses PETER's cheek, then pulls MOLLY's hair.*

Peter   Wizard!

Molly   My hair!

Ted   C'mere, you!

> *The Light vanishes down the beach. TED runs off after it.*

Prentiss   I can totally do that trick. *(turns and hollers)* Hey! Don't eat it, Teddy!

> *PRENTISS runs off after TED.*

Aster   *(pleased with himself)* Nice to know I've still got it.

Molly   If you really want to protect him, you'd take him with us.

Scott   *(from off)* Tide's going out, my Lord!

Aster   I'm afraid it's time for good-byes.

> *ASTER steps discreetly away. MOLLY pulls herself together.*

Molly   Be a woman. *(tears a label from inside her pinafore and hands it to PETER)* This is my address in London. You don't have to write me every day or anything, just when you feel like it.

Peter   Well — you know my address. Molly Island.

Molly Mollusk Island, you mean.

PETER notices the piece of shipwreck carved with the word NEVERLAND.

Peter Or maybe I'll call it "Neverland" – y'know, to remember. *(They both smile at that. PETER takes off his hat and places it on MOLLY's head.)* Hat of hero. Wear it when you get home.

Molly To remember.

Aster Molly, now. The tide won't wait.

Molly I want you to look after Prentiss and Teddy.

Peter Five more minutes! C'mon, a bedtime story! Tell me, Molly, tell me!

Molly *(to ASTER)* There'll be other tides, won't there?

Peter Y'see? She wants to stay!

Aster She can't.

Peter *(almost frantic)* But I don't want it to end!!

Aster Soon, Peter. You'll forget, and it won't hurt anymore.

Molly No! It's supposed to hurt – that's how you know it meant something! *(to PETER)* This isn't the end. You're going to remember everything, every single detail –

Peter And you're a better leader.

Molly Really?

Peter No.

They laugh, enjoying each other. Then it changes.

Molly You won't stay mad at me forever, will you?

Peter Go on, get lost.

Molly I'm bound to grow up, see? What would we do?

Peter Be friends.

Molly In a year, that'd be hard. In five years, it'd be silly. In twenty years, it would just be sad.

Peter   *(bitterly)* You sound older already.

> *MOLLY goes to her father. ASTER comforts her gently.*

Aster   The thing you did, against impossible odds – it's what the two of you will always have.

Peter   The thing we did . . .

Molly   Against impossible odds . . . *(deliberately comes back to PETER and kisses him on the mouth)* Yes, I wanted to.

> *MOLLY runs off. ASTER stops PETER from pursuing her, then exits. PETER is alone. A moment. Then the COMPANY enters, one by one.*

Narrator Scott   Peter watches the *Wasp* get smaller and smaller, wondering about his adventure, about Molly, about that kiss.

Narrator Stache   It would be the only moment that Peter would teeter, at the top of the rolley-coaster, on the verge of becoming what he'd always hated – a grown-up.

Narrator Aster   And then, as promised, he began to forget. And stayed right where he was.

Narrator Stache   The outsider.

Narrator Alf   Molly, true to her word, would remember everything, until one night, many years later –

Narrator Smee   – she stared out the nursery window watching Peter fly off with her daughter in tow –

Narrator Bumbrake   – and this grown-up Molly would comfort her new Nana, the good old dog who tended her children –

Narrator Molly   "Don't worry, Nana darling. I always hoped, if Peter came to visit, that my daughter would take my place. And once Wendy grows up – "

Narrator Fighting Prawn "I hope she will have a little girl – "

Narrator Hawking Clam "A little girl who will go off with him in turn – "

Narrator Bumbrake *(gently singing)*
OH, FOR THE WINGS,
FOR THE WINGS OF A DOVE . . .

Narrator Molly And so may we go on and on, dear Nana, as long as children are young and innocent –

Narrator Stache – and rude and juvenile and heartless –

Narrator Aster – past all of the jostles of life –

Narrator Molly – 'til we fly back home.

> *The singing ends. PETER has just what he always wanted.*

Peter Home.

> *A moment. TED and PRENTISS run on, ducking and swatting, pursued by the Light and the sound of bells.*

Ted HELP! That bird-bell thing is after us!!

Prentiss Keep it away! It's tryin' to eat my brains!!

Peter Over here! I'm the one you want!

Ted Get it away! Get it away!!

> *The Light flutters directly to PETER and speaks to him in Bell.*

Peter Okay, okay, calm down – I think . . . yeah, I think she wants me to race you down to the grotto.

Ted *(having spotted his pineapple)* Look! Stache sliced it open! *(finally able to gnaw on the fruit, blissful)* Oh, yes – mmm, OH YES!

Prentiss It's hard to believe you're still single.

Peter *(to the Light)* Wait! How can I race 'em to the grotto
  if I don't run?? Whoa whoa whoa – I can what???

    The Light flies off, zoom!

Prentiss What'd she say? What'd she say??

Peter "To have faith is to have wings."

    The COMPANY approaches and surrounds PETER.

Prentiss Wait a minute – did you say grotto?

Peter How'd you like to just be a boy for a while?

Ted The starstuff water can do that?

Peter It makes you what you want to be.

Prentiss A lawyer?

    The COMPANY slowly lifts PETER.

Peter Guys – this is gonna be one awfully big adventure.

Ted, Prentiss All right! You said it!

Peter Ready?

All READY!

Peter Set?

All SET!

Molly *(happy for her friend, she sets PETER free)* Go!

    Then, supported by the company, PETER shoots up
    from a crouch –

Peter *(crows)* Ca ca Ca ca CAAAH!

    – and flies!

    BLACKOUT.

TIRAMISU!